'We live in an age when noisy moralism is everywhere, and the news and social media have invaded the pulpit. Quiet reflection on moral truth, however, and the noble sobriety of public administration, have become under-valued virtues. All power to a book like this in redressing that imbalance.'

— *Matthew Parris,* Times *Columnist and Author*

'Social capital is the glue that holds communities together and it is a vital commodity in short supply. This book offers welcome recognition of those public servants and private citizens who recognise a moral imperative in working to make our society stronger.'

— *Mark Easton, BBC News Home Editor*

'The Westminster Abbey Institute helps the people who wander the four corners of Parliament Square where church, law and politics live together. And so does this book. Yet it can help more than this small community. It is both a challenging and caring read for leaders and managers everywhere. It avoids the easy temptation to preach, but offers a clear direction for those who will listen.'

— *Sir Bernard Hogan-Howe, Commissioner of the Metropolitan Police until 2017*

'Meet the better angels of your nature. Find out what "public service" really means.'

— *Lord Saatchi, Member of the House of Lords and Former Chairman of the Conservative Party*

'In this increasingly uncertain society of post truth in which we live, these lectures and discussions are thought-provoking and timely. They give the opportunity for reflection, particularly, for those who serve the public, in whatever capacity, to know where they stand and having found that place hold to it. Congratulations to the Westminster Abbey Institute.'

– Baroness Butler-Sloss, Member of the
House of Lords and Former President of the
Family Division of the High Court

'The conflict between moral courage, idealism and compromise…requires constant attention, and it is this struggle that keeps us morally alive and allows us to retain our souls. Through a combination of deep moral philosophy and historical perspectives, leavened by practical experience and revealed in compelling interviews, this book achieves something rather special: it forces us to think about who we are, what we do and why?'

– Baroness D'Souza, Scientist and
Member of the House of Lords

THE MORAL HEART OF PUBLIC SERVICE

of related interest

Morals, Rights and Practice in the Human Services
Effective and Fair Decision-Making in Health,
Social Care and Criminal Justice
Marie Connolly and Tony Ward
ISBN 978 1 84310 486 5
eISBN 978 1 84642 716 9

The Forgiveness Project
Stories for a Vengeful Age
Marina Cantacuzino
Forewords by Archbishop Emeritus
Desmond Tutu and Alexander McCall Smith
ISBN 978 1 78592 000 4
eISBN 978 1 78450 006 1

Learning from Baby P
The politics of blame, fear and denial
Sharon Shoesmith
ISBN 978 1 78592 003 5
eISBN 978 1 78450 238 6

THE MORAL HEART OF PUBLIC SERVICE

Edited by Claire Foster-Gilbert

Foreword by John Hall, Dean of Westminster
Afterword by Stephen Lamport

WESTMINSTER ABBEY
Institute

Jessica Kingsley *Publishers*
London and Philadelphia

First published in 2017
by Jessica Kingsley Publishers
73 Collier Street
London N1 9BE, UK
and
400 Market Street, Suite 400
Philadelphia, PA 19106, USA

www.jkp.com

Library of Congress Cataloging in Publication Data
A CIP catalog record for this book is available from the Library of Congress

British Library Cataloguing in Publication Data
A CIP catalogue record for this book is available from the British Library

ISBN 978 1 78592 255 8
eISBN 978 1 78450 540 0

Printed and bound in Great Britain

MIX
Paper from
responsible sources
FSC
www.fsc.org   FSC® C013056

CONTENTS

FOREWORD

John Hall, Dean of Westminster

Who is my neighbour? the lawyer asked Jesus. His answer was the parable of the Good Samaritan. The neighbour was the one who showed mercy to the wounded man left half dead by the roadside. That could be anyone, Jesus implied. The obvious neighbours, the Priest and Levite, had done nothing to help. The only one who helped came from a different religious and ethnic background. He was the neighbour. So proximity is not a key ingredient of neighbourliness. Our neighbour is not just the person next door.

Who is our neighbour, when 'our' means Westminster Abbey, the Dean and Chapter and all those engaged with us in our ministry? Jesus Christ's message would suggest that we look more widely than our immediate neighbours, those living or working next door to the Abbey. And we do. We welcome visitors and worshippers from almost every country in the world. We are pleased to receive heads of state and of government from around the world when they visit London. We have particularly lively links with the countries of the Commonwealth. We seek to draw into our fellowship those of other Christian denominations and those of other faiths as well as those of no particular religious faith. So we see the role of the Abbey as representing faith at the heart of the nation as a whole, and beyond.

'At the heart of the nation!' We do not presume to think of the Abbey itself as at the heart of the nation; rather, we think of the beating heart of the nation that sends the blood racing around the system of the body politic as the assembly of institutions that constitute public service. And many of these are our nearest neighbours in and around Parliament Square. The Abbey was here first, in AD 960, on a remote island surrounded by the Thames and its tributaries a mile and a half south of the City of London; a West Minster to compare with the East Minster of St Paul's Cathedral. But then these other various organs of the state gradually gathered around Westminster Abbey: Edward the Confessor's Palace of Westminster, the Houses of Parliament; St James's Palace and Buckingham Palace; the departments of state in and around Whitehall; in 2009, the Supreme Court on Parliament Square, replacing the judicial functions of the House of Lords; in Horse Guards, the London District of the British Army; and the Metropolitan Police headquarters.

The Westminster Abbey Institute we founded in 2013 to build a link with these immediate neighbours is based on a mutual concern to ponder deeply the holy and good, in the hope that together we could articulate the spiritual and moral values and virtues that should animate policy and administration. We have been encouraged and surprised by the response. We wish this volume now not just to preserve what has been offered but also to promote further responses.

ACKNOWLEDGEMENTS

The contributors to this volume would like to thank Jane Sinclair, Kathleen James, Natalie Watson, Ruth Cairns, Eleanor Lovegrove, Frances D'Souza, Westminster Abbey Institute's Council of Reference and the Dean and Chapter of Westminster for their support and encouragement.

Introduction

Claire Foster-Gilbert

A public service institution can be imagined as a sailing boat. If it is a government department, at the helm stands the Permanent Secretary, who, like all good helmsmen, seeks never to steer the boat more than five degrees either side of the compass direction upon which the boat is set. Civil servants in the department form the crew, from the navigator who must know the course and ensure the helmsman anticipates obstacles, to the scrubber of decks who ensures no one slips up. All have their part to play in ensuring the boat remains shipshape and able to withstand the waves and the winds in travelling its appointed course. The same dispensation of roles and tasks would apply by analogy to other institutions.

The waves are the events of the nation and the world. They may be relatively calm or they may rise into steep and stormy mountains of water, threatening the stability of the boat.

The winds are public opinion, which can fill the sails of the boat and send it scudding on its chosen course. They can gust and buffet, interrupting the boat's smooth journey. Or they can blow adversely, threatening to push the boat off course altogether.

Hence, the helmsman cannot simply hold the tiller fixedly. He or she must constantly adjust to respond to the wind and the waves, aiming to keep within five degrees either side of the compass direction or risk increasingly over-compensatory swings away from the course of travel.

The compass point towards which the boat is sailing is, variously interpreted, the good. As such, since we have never seen absolute goodness, it is not so much a destination as a direction of travel: the journey itself is what matters, not the arrival.

By whom is the good defined and the direction of travel therefore determined? For the government department, the minister is granted that responsibility and privilege by virtue of having been elected by universal franchise. (More broadly, governments set the direction of travel for all the institutions within the nation they govern.) In defining the good, ministers have to have their party's support. And of course the strength of the prevailing wind, public opinion, may be such as to determine a change of compass direction altogether. For the politician, public opinion will set parameters on what he or she can achieve. The great political leader will have a vision of the good that transcends narrow-minded concerns but retains party support and respects the parameters set by the prevailing wind of public opinion. The visionary and skilled politician will learn, quite possibly from his or her civil servants, about the art of tacking. Because of course it is the helmsman and the crew who execute the tack and any other sailing manoeuvres required. The civil service crew, having gathered the evidence – sniffed the wind, watched the waves – will need to be able to tell ministers when their proposed direction of travel will not work: when, whatever the ministers might want to think, their proposed direction is possibly not towards the good.

The point of the analogy is to show how dynamic and complex the art of public service is. The lazy assumption that 'people in public life are not moral' goes uncontested by too many of us, and it is not true, not of the vast majority of dedicated people who keep the ships of public service in all its forms on the move. But 'moral' is a word they shy away from. There is a kind of taboo around it, with the result that perfectly respectable moral disagreement subsides into a default assertion that every moral choice is equally valid and, by the same token, merely one lifestyle choice among many. There is no 'good' direction of travel; no visions beyond the horizon to pursue; only quotidian choices. This is a wholesale retreat from moral rigour, and it matters, very much indeed. We must not sleepwalk into national and global instability, fear and hate because we were afraid to defend what we believed to be right. If a boat has no clear direction to travel in, all that is really left for it to do is to keep afloat and not crash into anything else in the water. It finds its place only in relation to other boats. Its crew is busy, but not for any good reason.

We make moral choices all the time, whether we know it and own it or not. Every answer to the question 'What ought I to do?' has moral implications, from purchasing decisions to where we send our children to school, choices that seem personal, but are not. Public servants, including politicians and their clerks and advisers; civil servants; people in the uniformed, diplomatic and secret services; teachers; lawyers; clinicians; journalists and ministers of religion make moral choices that clearly implicate others all the time. Allowing moral thinking to subside into the unexamined silt of our visceral beings is thus, for public servants, particularly hazardous. But it can become a habit, born of the fear of being seen as a moralizer; as an imposer of moral judgements on others; and also of getting it wrong.

There is historical force behind this habit. Politicians look back with haunted eyes at their predecessors who tried to speak of society's moral reawakening and were dragged into the mire for their efforts as the media gleefully found the skeletons in their cupboards. The consequence is lack of vision and the boat sails towards an unknown horizon, blown about by the changing winds of public opinion and the waves of economic unease, ecological crisis and warring peoples. Civil servants look back with haunted eyes at the career-limiting errors of judgement of their colleagues who were then briefed against by their ministers or who tried to speak truth to power and were cut by their ministers. For good reason, they choose instead to avoid bringing up the moral dilemmas all policy-making entails, using their intelligence to make the policy look coherent and make the minister happy, silencing the quiet voice that whispers reminders of historical slippery slopes into tyrannical regimes administered by efficient officials who also did not vest themselves in a mantle of moral responsibility. They concentrate on keeping the ship afloat and do not look up to see where it is heading. Risk aversion threatens moral courage in the armed and unarmed forces; teachers can feel forced to teach to the test; journalists to tell the story that is too good to check; ministers of religion mumble uninspiring texts for fear of upsetting anyone. We are all guilty of the moral laziness that is born of fear.

And we all have skeletons, if not put in our cupboards ourselves then by our more interesting relatives. And everyone makes more or less imperfect moral decisions. What everyone also has, however, is a moral sense, which is kept alive not least by our awareness of our fallibility. Moral health, like physical health, has to be consciously maintained. The humility of self-knowledge is a start, but, like the regular exercise and good diet that follow from knowing how unfit we are, that same moral humility should give rise to attending to those things that keep our moral judgement reasonable and our responses to other people and the planet loving, attentive and true. We learn and re-learn how to choose compass directions that are oriented towards the good, and we practise the dynamic responsive helming that keeps us on course. We remain attentive to the ever-changing wind and waves. We take turns to keep watch.

This volume of essays and dialogues is based upon lectures given at Westminster Abbey Institute, where the listening stillness of the Abbey's porous medieval walls have heard a thousand years of heartfelt pleas for help in 'getting it right'. Westminster Abbey Institute was established in 2013 to revitalize moral and spiritual values in public life and service, working particularly with the public servants in the institutions of government and other forms of public service around Parliament Square: the Abbey's neighbours. The geography is pertinent: with the Houses of Parliament to the east, the Treasury and all of Whitehall to the north and the Supreme Court to the west, we have legislature, executive, judiciary on three sides, and the spiritual powerhouse of the

Abbey to the south, on standby to support and nourish the public service that is offered on the other three sides.

The essays seek to make the Abbey's walls speak: they are a bid to provide inspiration and method to orient our public servants' moral ships' compasses and kindle their moral strength in keeping on course. The essays do not provide a solid bulwark of moral certainty, because the helmsman must be free to adjust his or her steering, but rather seek to make the conscience of the public servant restless in the search for greater understanding of what the good is that we are all trying to reach towards, of what it means to serve; to reconnect with the vocation to public service; to recognize and stay alive to the moral dilemmas inherent in public service of all kinds; to work together to that end.

The first essay is by former Foreign Secretary William Hague, who writes of the different experience of speaking in Westminster Abbey, where he is not timed, rushed or interrupted and has a decent chance of being listened to and having his listeners reflect at leisure upon his words, from speaking in the Commons where none of those things necessarily pertains. The essay is a good place to start: Hague explores the role of Britain in the world as a moral force, lifting our eyes beyond the horizon of national self-interest and seeing how we can be of service internationally. 'Restless' in the title of this essay should be understood as not settled or certain or complete. Paradoxically, the conscience can remain restless when it feels safe to question and does not feel it needs to take refuge in dogma.

The three essays that follow, by Claire Foster-Gilbert, offer tools for growing moral courage. The first essay provides a framework of goal-based, duty-based and right-based questions for analysing a moral decision, showing how it is that most decisions cannot be morally perfect and what, precisely, the moral cost of any decision might be. All actions have goals, and the first question to be addressed is the value and importance of that goal, but a good goal is not enough to justify an action. Will important moral principles, such as not lying or not harming, be sacrificed to achieve the goal? And what do those most affected by the decision feel about it? If the end seems right and the means are not harmful, but stakeholders do not want it, what then?

The second essay draws back from moral analysis to moral perception, looking at the way we see the world, exploring the values that we dearly hold. The suggestion is that right perception involves seeing that all things are interconnected, that all things have intrinsic value and not just value because of their usefulness and that we have to stop rushing about in order to see that this is so. Working towards such perceptions gives rise to a deep love, which is the best moral perception of all. If we love, we will act well towards each other, far better than if we simply know more; for while the growth of knowledge increases power, the growth of love increases service.

In the third essay, recognizing that moral courage is earned through character development, the reader is taken on a 'hero's journey' from hearing a call out of his or her ordinary world, questioning the call, meeting a mentor who gives courage to cross the threshold on to the journey, facing trials and overcoming them, making mistakes, learning who are allies and who enemies, facing the darkest time when everything has gone wrong, facing a great ordeal, claiming the prizes and going on to a new level of life as a servant leader, having learned the lessons of the journey, the chief of which is, perhaps, that the journey is not about the so-called hero but about everyone else. The journey has to be taken for this knowledge to dawn: there are no shortcuts to the growing of moral character.

Mary McAleese, former President of Ireland, in dialogue with John Hall, Dean of Westminster, describes with lyrical wisdom the painful participatory experience of bringing together people who have hated each other for centuries and, in her words, 'missed each other by a mile'. 'We interrogate ourselves, not each other, and learn our own failings, instead of gaining doctorates in each others'.' Her yearning for peace sings through her prose. She took no shortcuts. Her shrewd sense of the vital role of politics in achieving it is a manual for any who feel in themselves the call to serve through these means.

Vernon White's three essays on the theme of idealism and compromise explore how we are kept morally alive by our constant failure to live up to our ideals while at the same time finding that we are unable to renounce them. Compromise is contextualized by idealism and is its foil: understanding it as such means we will stretch our moral and spiritual fibre beyond what we think we can achieve. In his second essay, White demonstrates profound self-awareness in his observation that the force of moral energy is misplaced into loud denunciations of others' behaviours because moral relativism means we no longer trust its direction. This is an observation made on the way to his principal argument that the moral impulse, always calling us to see more need than we can ever hope to meet, carries the quality of the infinite. But rather than being permanently distressed by voracious moral demand, somewhat surprisingly we can relax: relax into the realization that we cannot, alone, meet all our ideals and, when we fail, we need not adopt a self-regarding tragedic heroic justification but should continue to pursue the real goal of our original endeavour. Purposefulness, explored in White's third essay, refuses to be put down, as he shows: it survives even the most persistent setbacks. Such staying power indicates the existence of a wider narrative, the full extent and depth of which we cannot see. In this understanding of purpose, successes and failures are not indicators of progress or its lack, but dynamic movements within a cosmic narrative in which we play our part.

Westminster Abbey is a Benedictine Foundation dating from 960, when a small group of monks arrived on Thorney Island under the patronage of King Edgar and St Dunstan. Rowan Williams sets the Foundation to work, as it were, in service of Parliament Square, which has grown around it. He draws on the Benedictine vow of stability, describing it as 'not going away'. The crew, to return to the analogy at the beginning of this Introduction, will not abandon ship. Nor, importantly, will it be assumed that difficulties can be solved by making the stranger walk the plank. He or she is not going away either. The Benedictine Rule identifies honesty, peace and accountability as critical to the health of any community: honesty in our dealings with others and our own self-awareness; peace sustained not falsely by avoiding conflict, but authentically by paying close attention to everyone's needs; and accountability particularly of the abbess or abbot to the particular skills and gifts of the members of the community. Williams asks: what is the currency of any institution or community, which is to say, what do people in the group talk about when they see each other in the corridors, in the coffee breaks (in the galley and companionway)? Often, and tellingly, the currency is grievance, and that is not healthy.

The following three essays offer further treasures from the Benedictine tradition, with interpretations of three Benedictine virtues of stability, community and conversion of manners, for public service in the twenty-first century. Vernon White characterizes stability as 'creative fidelity'. He points to the many destabilizing forces that can undermine a secure sense of self and belonging and can make us vulnerable to fundamentalist political or religious ideologies that falsely promise security. Fidelity means faithfulness over time to people and institutions; it is creative because the constancy is at the same time challenging, harnessing change to deal with the change we see in others and in ourselves as we walk alongside one another, 'not going away'. There is resilience to be found in a symbiotic rather than an opposing relationship between Heraclitus' flux and Parmenides' constancy. Stability can be a casualty of modern liberalism, but not if it is a call to a progressive, life-giving, healing and dynamic disposition of person and institution.

Andrew Tremlett offers a detailed historical, etymological and social analysis of 'community'. He draws lessons from the tough and counter-cultural call the monk hears to join a monastic community and the efforts that are made to put him off. A strong community calls for intentional communion, hard work and sacrificial living. Tremlett convincingly demonstrates how much the communities of Westminster and Whitehall: Parliament, the judiciary and government departments, not just the Abbey itself, have a strong ethos and culture, and their members have a sense of vocation and loyalty to the cause and purpose of their institutions.

In the third essay, Claire Foster-Gilbert draws upon the imponderable 'conversion of manners' of which Benedict writes, understanding it as a readiness to re-convert: regularly heading out to the metaphorical desert to re-tune, re-member and be ready to allow paradigms to shift and new connections to be made, aware that the first conversion (strong desire to make a difference, save the world, etc.) can be the greatest enemy of the second. Morality is dynamic, and so should we be.

Peter Hennessy, in conversation with Claire Foster-Gilbert, leaves us with the sweetest note, however. In a conversation that took place amidst the profoundly destabilizing political events of 2016, he sings the Benedictine threnodies that run through this volume of stability, intentionality and purpose. He lauds the public service that does not shout about itself, that takes its place in the company of all those who have gone before and will follow, playing its part, unsung and for the most part unknown. He wonders if a memorial for the 'unknown public servant' should stand in Westminster Abbey. There is one, recently laid, for the security services of MI5, MI6 and GCHQ. It and the older Grave of the Unknown Warrior are fitting comparators for and an explicit acknowledgement of what public service really is. The most important, most morally sensitive and courageous service is often that which will never be seen.

The essays and dialogues can be read individually or as a collection. They will appeal in different ways. None is intended to moralize, rather to share the skill, the effort, the camaraderie and the humour involved in making robust moral decisions, in everything that is involved in sailing the ship towards a good destination, which should, after all, be seen as a profound and defining human endeavour for us all.

Humanizing Hell

Our Restless Conscience
and the Search for Peace

William Hague

This essay is based upon the One People Oration I delivered at Westminster Abbey in October 2014. I have made hundreds of speeches in the House of Commons as a Member of Parliament for 25 years, but this was the only one I had given in Westminster Abbey. In its early days, in the early 1300s, Parliament actually sat there, in the Chapter House and then in the Refectory of the Abbey. So as an MP I felt very at home, but there were important differences. The Commons is a scene of noisy disagreement, while in the Abbey we were surrounded by a thousand years of reflection and calm. In the Commons I would be cut off mid-flow if I went a minute over my allotted time, but in the Abbey I spoke for as long as I needed to and had some hope the audience might actually have been listening. When I spoke in the House of Commons I was just yards from where my hero William Pitt the Younger (Hague 2005) debated with Fox and Burke and Sheridan, but he was actually buried in the Abbey, with his father, in what I believe is the only grave in our country to contain two prime ministers.

People often comment that politicians are becoming younger, but Pitt was prime minister at the age of 24. There has never been a younger occupant of Number 10 before or since, and I doubt there will ever be one again or one as peculiarly gifted as a parliamentary orator. Pitt was prime minister for 18 years and 11 months, and for half that time Britain was at war with France and frequently at risk of invasion.

Another hero of mine, William Wilberforce (Hague 2008), is also buried in the Abbey, thanks to his family and friends countermanding his wish to be buried elsewhere. His house, Number 4 Palace Yard, stood just over the wall and was by every account a veritable pandemonium of books, pets, visitors and hapless servants he never had the heart to let go. From amid that ferment of ideas and activity he spent 20 years converting the people and entire political establishment of Britain to the cause of abolition. Year after year he moved motions in the House of Commons that were defeated. But in 1807, two decades after he began, he finally succeeded in turning our country from a slave-trading nation into one that bullied, harassed and bribed other countries into giving up their own detestable traffic in humans. And he did this without ever holding any office in any government.

Although I am not an intensely religious person, in writing my book on Wilberforce I came to admire the unquenchable determination to succeed in a cause that religion – in his case evangelical Christianity – inspired in him. Because he believed he was accounting to God for how he spent his time, he actually recorded what he did with it. His papers include tables detailing each quarter hour of the day. One typical entry describes seven and a half hours of Commons business, eight and a quarter hours in bed, five and a half hours of 'requisite company &c visits &c', three-quarters of an hour of serious reading and meditation, 15 minutes unaccounted for or dressing and one hour described as 'squandered'.

While few in his age had his gift with words and his obsessive drive, Wilberforce was not alone in being inspired by his faith. He was part of the Clapham sect, a small group of politicians, lawyers, merchants, churchmen and bankers based around Clapham Common, who were responsible for one of the greatest varieties and volumes of charitable activity ever launched by any group of people in any age. Their primary goal was the abolition of the slave trade and the founding of Sierra Leone, but on top of this they set up a staggering array of charitable causes: the London Missionary Society; the Society for Bettering the Condition and Increasing the Comforts of the Poor; the Church Missionary Society; the Religious Tract Society; the Society for Promoting the Religious Instruction of Youth; the Society for the Relief of the Industrious Poor; the British National Endeavour for the Orphans of Soldiers and Sailors; the Institution for the Protection of Young Girls; the Society for the Suppression of Vice; the Sunday School Union; the Society for Superceding the Necessity for Climbing Boys in Cleansing Chimneys; the British and Foreign Bible Society; and two with particularly wonderful names: The Asylum House of Refuge for the Reception of Orphaned Girls the

Settlements of whose Parents Cannot be Found and, finally, the Friendly Female Society, for the Relief of Poor, Infirm, Aged Widows, and Single Women of Good Character, Who Have Seen Better Days. And we think *we* live in an age of activism.

I know that for many people today religious faith of all kinds remains a great inspiration and channel for charity and altruism. And whatever faith or creed we live by, inherent in our democracy is the idea that our freedoms and rights are universal. Oppression or conflict or poverty or injustice anywhere in the world has stirred our consciences, as individuals and collectively, throughout our history. I want to argue that maintaining and building on that national tradition is absolutely vital in the twenty-first century, both as a moral obligation and in order to prevent wars at a time of growing international instability.

The year 2014, when I delivered my lecture in Westminster Abbey, saw us marking 100 years since the First World War, in which so many of our countrymen perished because conflict was not averted. Remembering that dreadful conflict should inspire us to maintain our restless conscience as a nation and be determined to do whatever we can to improve the condition of humanity. We should have faith – in the broadest sense – in our ideas and our ideals as a country, and in our ability to have a positive impact on the development of other nations and the future of our world.

One of the most moving sights I have seen in some time was the sea of poppies encircling the Tower of London, commemorating each and every British and Commonwealth military fatality in the First World War. It was a silent exhortation to remember, to be grateful for what we have and to learn the lessons of those times when peace had to be restored at so great a price to humanity. So too is the revered Grave of the Unknown Warrior in Westminster Abbey, 'buried among Kings', as his gravestone says, as one of the many who 'gave the most that man can give, life itself, for God, for King and Country, for Loved Ones and Empire, for the Sacred Cause of Justice and the Freedom of the World'. The remains of 15 British soldiers from the War were reburied in Belgium in October 2014, 100 years after they were killed in battle, reminding us that we are still counting the cost of that terrible conflagration.

As Foreign Secretary, for four years I occupied the office used by Sir Edward Grey, with its windows overlooking Horseguards and St James's Park. Standing at those windows, as he contemplated the catastrophe about to engulf the world, he famously said, 'the lamps are going out all over Europe; we shall not see them lit again in our lifetime'. The failure of diplomacy on the eve of the War ushered in greater suffering than Grey and his contemporaries could ever have imagined: war on an industrial scale, 'the butchery of the unknown by the unseen', in the words of one war correspondent, in which 10 million soldiers died on all sides, 20 million were severely wounded and eight million were permanently disabled; in which appalling massacres, rapes and other atrocities were committed against thousands of civilians and millions of refugees were created; and which was all to be followed by the Second World War, the massacres in Poland, the gas chambers and extermination camps of the Holocaust, pogroms in the Soviet Union and the slaughter of war and revolution in China.

It is tempting to look back on the horrors and evils of the past and to think that these things could not happen again. It would be comforting to imagine that we have reached such a level of education and enlightenment that ideologies like Nazism, Fascism and Communism that led to mass slaughter, and the nationalism that leads states to attack their neighbours or groups within states to massacre their fellow citizens, have all seen an end. Sadly, I believe this is an illusion.

There is an additional illusion that sometimes takes hold, as it did before the First World War, that a permanent peace has arrived. Then, Europe had enjoyed 99 years without widespread war. The Great Powers had found a way back from the brink of conflict several times, and Grey and his colleagues can be forgiven for thinking that crises would always be resolved by diplomacy, when in fact they were on the edge of the two greatest cataclysms in history.

History shows that while circumstances change, human nature is immutable. However educated, advanced or technologically skilled we become, we are still highly prone to errors of judgement, to greed and thus to conflict. There is no irreversible progress towards democracy, human rights and greater freedoms just as there is unlikely to be any such thing as a state of permanent peace. Unless each generation acts to preserve the gains it inherits and to build upon them for the future, then peace, democracy and freedom can easily be eroded, and conflict can readily break out.

It is true that there is more education, welfare, charitable endeavour and kindness in our world than ever before, that we have reached extraordinary diplomatic milestones like the Nuclear Non-Proliferation Treaty and that we have a United Nations (UN) system carrying out responsibilities from peacekeeping to the protection of our environment. We should never lose faith in the positive side of human nature and always retain our optimism and belief in our ability to shape our destiny. But my argument is that it is also true that the capacity of human beings to inflict unspeakable violence upon others, of ideologies that are pure evil to rise up or for states that are badly led to wade into new forms of conflict are all as present as ever.

We often read about massacres as if such barbaric things are only to be found in the pages of history. But the short span of our own lifetimes tells a different story, from Europe to the Middle East, to Africa and Asia. Only in 1995, in Europe, 8000 men and boys were massacred in Srebrenica in a single week. Over five million people have been killed in the Congo in the two decades up to 2014. In April 2014, when I attended the 20th anniversary of the Rwandan massacres, I and the other international representatives were standing where nearly a third of a million people are buried in a single grave, a third of the million women, men and children slain in cold blood within 100 days. Also in 2014, two of Pol Pot's henchmen, part of the Khmer Rouge regime that killed more than a million people, were convicted and given life sentences. In Iraq and Syria, in a perversion of religion, ISIL (Islamic State of Iraq and the Levant) is currently terrorizing communities with beheadings and crucifixions. And think of the barrel bombs that have rained down on schools in Syria from the Assad regime and the pitiless desperation to hold on to power needed to produce such utter inhumanity.

Aggressive ideology, despotism and fanaticism live on, despite all our other advances and achievements. This is the human condition. Our optimism and faith in human nature will always have to contend with this harsh truth, at the same time as being essential to overcoming such evils. That is why it is so important for us to have a strong sense of history so that we never lose sight of how fragile peace and security can be. And so we understand that diplomacy and the peaceful resolution of conflicts is not an abstract concept but our greatest responsibility.

In our information-rich, media-saturated world, history can be caricatured as a luxury, not least for those who have their hands full running the country. But I could not imagine having been Foreign Secretary without drawing on the advice of the Foreign Office historians, who were able to offer historical precedents for every conceivable revolution, insurgency, treaty or crisis, and who produced maps and papers that shed light on the most intractable of modern problems. It is as important to consult the lessons of history in foreign policy as it is to seek the advice of our embassies, our intelligence agencies, our military and our allies. History is not set in stone and is open to endless reinterpretation. But the habit of deep and searching thought rooted in history must be cultivated: not to paralyse us or make us excessively pessimistic, but to help us make sound decisions and guide our actions.

It remains as true today as it was when Edmund Burke first expressed it that the only thing necessary for evil to triumph is for good men and women to do nothing. We cannot in our generation coast along or think it is not our responsibility or that it is too difficult to tackle conflict and injustice that bring misery to millions. However pressing the crises of the day, we have to address the fundamental conditions that lead to armed conflict and reduce the human suffering it causes. This means not only maintaining Britain's global role – living up to our responsibilities, protecting our interests internationally and being able to project military power where necessary – but also consciously encouraging and developing the ideas, concepts and strategies needed to address poverty, conflict and injustice.

All our advances start with an idea. Powerful ideas can then become unstoppable movements as indeed the abolition of the slave trade did in the eighteenth century. For that to happen governments have to adopt the best of these ideas, and leaders have to be prepared to be open and radical.

The title of my essay is taken from a remark by Admiral John Fisher, First Sea Lord in the early nineteenth century and commander of the Royal Navy at the start of the First World War. In 1899, he was sent as Britain's representative to the first Hague Peace Conference, called by Russia, to discuss the growing arms race and place curbs on the use of certain weapons in war. As these proposals were discussed at the negotiating table, he is said to have remarked with some passion that one could sooner talk of 'humanizing hell' than of 'humanizing war'. While he was, of course, right about the hell of war, in actual fact the traumatic experience of conflict and great idealism have often gone together. It has frequently been the very experience of war that has spurred mankind's greatest advances in international relations, based on ideas that were radical when first presented. When Henry Dunant observed the agonizing deaths of thousands of injured men at the battle of Solferino in 1859, his outrage and activism led to the 1864 Geneva Convention, the founding text of contemporary international humanitarian law, which laid the foundation for the treatment of prisoners in war. After the First World War, there was a vast and intensive period of institution building, leading to the League of Nations, International Labour Organization, the prohibition on use of chemical weapons and the creation of the High Commissioner for Refugees to find a way of returning millions of European refugees to their homes, which supports over 50 million refugees and displaced people worldwide today.

While the Second World War was raging, Roosevelt and Churchill spent hours discussing the creation of a new international body to prevent conflict in the future, which led to the United Nations itself, the Security Council and the Universal Declaration of Human Rights. More recently, in our lifetime, the outrage at atrocities in Cambodia, Rwanda, Liberia and Bosnia led to the creation of the International Criminal Court and the concept of the Responsibility to Protect. Since 1990 our country has played a leading role in securing international bans on the use of cluster munitions and landmines, and I was proud to sign on Britain's behalf the ratification of the International Arms Trade Treaty, the culmination of ten years of advocacy begun here in Britain.

The humanizing of the hell of war is a continual process. While our goal must always be to avert conflict in the first place, except as a last resort as provided in the UN charter, it is also essential to establish norms of behaviour about what is unacceptable even in times of war. This is vital so that if conflict breaks out despite our best efforts, governments feel restrained by the threat of accountability for any crimes that are committed, we have mechanisms to protect civilians and peace agreements take account of the need for reconciliation and the punishment of crimes against humanity. The crucial point is that while the international bodies we have are the result of diplomacy, they do not simply arise on their own. They are the product of ideas generated by individuals, groups or governments refusing to accept the *status quo*, such that then, with enough momentum, public support and political commitment became reality.

I think of this 'restless conscience', as I call it, as an enduring and admirable British characteristic. Our non-governmental organizations (NGOs), lawyers, academics and Crown servants have had an extraordinary impact internationally. In my time in the Foreign Office I found our diplomats a powerful part of this tradition, from their work on the abolition of the death penalty, to improving the lot of lesbian, gay, bisexual and transgender (LGBT) communities worldwide, to helping negotiations as far away as the now-successful Mindanao Peace Process in the Philippines. This is part of our country's distinctive contribution to the world, and it involves the power of our ideas as much as the skill of our diplomats. We must always cherish and encourage that flow of ideas and idealism and those rivers of soft power and influence that form such a large part of our role in the world.

It is also true that diplomatic negotiations for peace do not simply arise automatically. They require extraordinary effort by individuals. US former Secretary of State, John Kerry, for example, deserves praise for his tireless work on the Israeli–Palestinian conflict. He chose to devote weeks on end trying to restart and conclude those negotiations, rather than taking the easy route of not attempting such a difficult task. Individuals and the choices they make have an immense impact. Sometimes the individual is someone in high office, like William Pitt, who did his utmost in the early 1790s to avoid war with France and whose State Paper of 1805 was the basis for European peace for most of the nineteenth century. Or it is someone like Wilberforce, who was never a government minister, but whose ideas and energy brought relief, an end of suffering and ultimately freedom for millions of people.

Choices are motivated differently. The coalition to end the British slave trade was driven not just by moral considerations, but also by political and economic factors.

Adam Smith argued against slavery because he saw it as an inefficient allocation of resources. British naval supremacy in the world meant that in simple political terms, abolition was possible because we had the diplomatic and military muscle to enforce it. And Wilberforce was outraged that slaves had no opportunity to embrace Christianity, so their souls were being lost. So his key argument against the trade was neither economic nor political, it was religious. It is inevitable that in this way governments, like individuals, are motivated by a number of different factors. But we must pursue the issues today that bring together the moral interest and the national interest, using the combination of powerful ideas, our strong institutions and our global role.

We should be proud that, so far, our country has kept its promise to spend 0.7 per cent of gross domestic product (GDP) on international development, not just because it is morally right, but also because it is profoundly in our national interest to help other nations lift their citizens out of poverty. We have to continue to lead global efforts to stop the illegal wildlife trade, which destroys the natural heritage of African nations, undermines economic development and creates instability. It is vital that we promote a rules-based international system, because it nourishes the commerce, trade and stability that are the lifeblood of our own economy as well as strengthening human rights internationally. And it is essential that we support political reform, civil society, women's rights and economic progress in the Middle East, because it is vital to our long-term security that that region becomes more free, more stable and more prosperous.

The pursuit of policies that bring stability in the world, and the moral authority for them, are inseparable. Any idea that we should retrench, withdraw or turn away from these issues is misguided and wrong for two reasons. First, the world is becoming systemically less stable. This is due to many different factors: the dispersal of power amongst a wider group of nations, many of whom do not fully share our values and our objectives in foreign policy; the diffusion of power away from governments, accelerated by technology; the globalization of ideas and ability of people to organize themselves into leaderless movements and spread ideas around the world within minutes; our interconnectedness, a boon for development but also a major vulnerability to threats, from terrorism and cyber crime to the spread of diseases like Ebola; the growing global middle class, which is driving demand for greater accountability and more freedom within states designed to suppress such instincts; and the rise of religious intolerance in the Middle East. Global institutions are struggling to deal with these trends. It is not enough to ensure there is no conflict on our own continent, although sadly the crisis in Ukraine has shown, once again, that even Europe is not immune. Conflict anywhere in the world affects us through refugee flows, the crimes and terrorism that conflict fuels and the billions of pounds needed in humanitarian assistance, so we have to address these issues.

Second, the pursuit of sound development, inclusive politics and the rule of law are essential to our moral standing in the world, which is in turn an important factor in our international influence. As I pointed out in 2006, the US and UK suffered a loss of moral authority as a result of aspects of the War on Terror, which affected the standing of our foreign policy and the willingness of other countries to work with us, and which both President Obama's administration and our own government worked hard to address. We are strongest when we act with moral authority, and that means being the strongest champions of our values.

Thus, neither as a matter of wise policy nor as a matter of conscience can Britain ever afford to turn aside from a global role. We have to continue to be restless advocates for improving the condition of humanity. This means continuing to forge new alliances, reforming the UN and other global institutions and enforcing the rules that govern international relations. But that will never be enough by itself, so we also have to retain the ambition to influence not just the resolutions that are passed and the treaties that are signed up to, but also the beliefs in the world about what is acceptable and what is not.

A powerful example of an issue on which we need to apply such leadership is the use of rape and sexual violence as weapons of war. I have been surprised by how deeply engrained and passive attitudes to this subject often are. Because history is full of accounts of the mass abuse of women and captives, and because there is so much domestic violence in all societies, it is a widely held view that violence against women and girls is inevitable in peacetime and in conflict. But when we see ISIL foreign fighters in Iraq and Syria selling women as slaves and glorifying rape and sexual slavery; when we hear of refugees, who have already lost everything, being raped in camps for want of basic protections; when we see leaders exhorting their fighters to go out and rape their opponents, specifically to inflict terror, to make women pregnant, to force people to flee their homes and to destroy their families and communities; or peace agreements giving amnesty to men who have ordered and carried out rape or deliberately turned a blind eye to it; or soldiers – and even peacekeepers – committing rape due to lack of discipline, proper training, no accountability and a culture that treats women as the spoils of war, a commodity to be exploited with impunity, then we are clearly dealing with injustice on a scale that is simply intolerable, as well as damaging to the stability of those countries and the peace of the wider world.

It is often said to me that without war there would be no warzone rape, as if that is the only way to address the problem. While of course our goal is always to prevent conflict, we cannot simply consign millions of women, men, girls and boys to the suffering of rape while we seek a way to put an end to all conflict, since, as I have argued, this goal is one we should always strive for but may often not attain.

We have shown that we can put restraints on the way war is conducted. We have put beyond the pale the use of poison gas or torture and devised the Arms Trade Treaty for the trade in illegal weapons. It is time to address this aspect of conflict and to treat sexual violence as an issue of global peace and security. The biggest obstacle we face in this campaign is the idea you cannot do anything about it – that you cannot humanize hell, that there is nothing we can do to end warzone rape. But there is hope, and we must dispel this pessimism. Over the last two years, working with NGOs, the UN and faith groups, we have brought the weight and influence of Britain to bear globally as no country ever has done before on this subject.

Over 150 countries have joined our campaign and endorsed a global declaration of commitment to end sexual violence in conflict. We brought together over 120 governments and thousands of people at a Global Summit in London in June 2014, the first of its kind. And in countries like the Democratic Republic of Congo, South Sudan and Colombia we are seeing signs of governments being prepared to address this issue by passing laws and reforming their militaries.

What would it say about our commitment to human rights in our own society if we knew about such abuses but did nothing about them? And how could we be at the forefront of preventing conflict in the world if we did not act to prevent something that causes conflict in the future? Sexual violence is often designed to make peace impossible to achieve and create the bitterness and incentive for future conflict. Dealing with it is not a luxury to be added on, it is an integral part of conflict prevention, a crucial part of breaking a cycle of war. And it has to go hand in hand with seeking the full political, social and economic empowerment of women everywhere, the greatest strategic prize of all for our century.

In 2014 we commemorated those who died in the First World War and their suffering. There is no more fitting thing we can do for the sake of that memory than to face up to the hell of conflict in our lifetimes. We have never had to mobilize our population to fight in the way their generation did, and so we have been spared their painful burdens. But how much more incumbent does that make it on all of us to fight with the peaceful tools at our disposal on behalf of those who are denied, through no fault of their own, the security we consider our birthright.

Just as in Wilberforce's day, it will always be necessary for Britain to be at the forefront of efforts to improve the condition of humanity. The search for peace and an end to conflict requires powerful ideas and the relentless defence of our values, as much it does negotiations and summits between nations. We could be heading for such turbulent times that it will be easy for some people to say we should not bother with development or tackling sexual violence in conflict or other such issues. There will always be the pressing crisis of the day that risks drowning out such long-term causes. But, in fact, addressing these issues is crucial to overcoming crises now and in the future – and it will be an increasingly important part of our moral authority and standing in the world that we are seen to do this.

Just because there are economic crises and major social changes does not mean we or our partners can squander any day or any year in producing the ideas as well as the laws that prevent conflict and deal with some of the greatest scourges of the twenty-first century, and we must do so with confidence: for it remains the case that free and democratic societies are the only places where the ideas and the moral force we need can be found. Our times call for a renewal of that effort – for just and equitable solutions to conflict, the driving down of global inequalities and the confronting of injustices.

Every day we have to start again: there is not going to be a day in our lifetimes when we can wake up and say this work is complete. We have to overcome the sense of helplessness that says that vast problems cannot be tackled. We have to awaken the conscience of nations and stir the actions of governments. In an age of mass communication this is a task for every one of us. Whether we are in government, are diplomats, journalists, members of the armed forces, members of the public, students, faith groups or civil servants, every one of us is part of that effort. In Britain, our restless conscience should never allow us to withdraw behind our fortifications and turn away from the world but should always inspire us to strive for peace and security, to maintain our responsibilities, seek new ways of addressing the worst aspects of human behaviour and live up to our greatest traditions.

Strengthening Moral Courage in Public Life

Three Essays by Claire Foster-Gilbert

Introduction

Where is moral courage to be found? Not just in intellectual rigour, though it is certainly there. Neither is it only in deep convictions, nor simply in passionate action. Moral courage is found in a combination of all three. This group of essays offers ways into each of these aspects. The first provides a framework for moral analysis, the second attends to the ways we perceive and therefore act in the world around us and the third takes the reader on an active 'hero's journey' into moral strength of character. They might be characterized thus: the first is for those who know they have to do the right thing but want to know how to work out what that is. The second is for those who feel they need encouragement to want to do the right thing. The third is for those who want to, and know what to do, but are hesitating on the threshold of action itself.

I should make it clear from the outset that when I argue for strengthening moral courage I am categorically not arguing for the kind of narrow moral certainty that ignores others and forges ahead regardless. Moral courage should be restless, constantly searching for what is the right thing to do, recognizing that events and people change and so should our thinking and acting. Like the helmsman steering a boat according to a compass, constantly adjusting in response to the wind and the waves so as to stay within five degrees of the direction of travel, we should remain wide awake and sensitive to the world around us and never think we have, finally, got it right. But we must choose to steer the boat in a particular direction and we have to be decisive at critical moments. A restless conscience is not to be taken as an excuse for procrastination.

I use 'moral' and 'ethical' synonymously: they are the Latin-influenced and Greek-influenced words for the same designation.

MORAL ANALYSIS

Introduction

In this essay, I will suggest a three-legged approach to moral analysis of goal-based, duty-based and right-based reasoning (Foster 2001), giving the pedigree of each of the three approaches and explaining why, like a three-legged stool, all three are needed, even though we may temperamentally or habitually prefer one over the other two. I will then offer some examples of its application to issues that arise for public servants and public service institutions. Finally, I will say why I think rigorous moral analysis is courageous.

Goal-based morality

The first leg of the three-legged approach is goal-based morality. This approach rests on the idea that actions are right if their outcomes are right, and at its most straightforward, 'right' means that more people are made happy than sad. On its own, goal-based morality has a refreshing simplicity. Its chief proponent was the famous philosopher Jeremy Bentham, who was a great thinker but had some strange habits that indicate someone attuned to what Iain McGilchrist (2009) calls the left-brain approach.

He did not get on with women at all, but he did give names to some of the inanimate objects that populated his life: his stick was called Dapple and his teapot, priapically, Dick. People set their watches by his daily walks. He left his body to University College London (UCL), not for scientific purposes, but to be stuffed and brought out to join college dinners so that people could see him and be reminded of the, as he called it, felicity principle. You can see his body even now on display in the Great Hall entrance of UCL.

It is not surprising to discover, then, that he disliked messy thinking. Trying to gain agreement on moral principles led, he believed, to messy thinking. We will not always agree whether it is more important not to lie than not to steal, but no one would disagree, whatever their religion, background or education, that pleasure is good and pain is bad. Bentham argued that notions of religious morality, commands from God, moral principles and values that may or may not be shared by others unhelpfully complicate moral decision-making. Of one thing only we can be certain: that people do not want pain and they do want pleasure. He wrote:

> Nature has placed mankind under the governance of two sovereign masters, pain and pleasure. It is for them alone to point out what we ought to do, as well as to determine what we shall do... By the principle of utility is meant that principle which approves or disapproves of every action whatsoever, according to the tendency which it appears to have to augment or diminish the happiness of the party whose interest is in question. (Bentham 1962, p.33, first published 1789)

So an action is right if it increases pleasure and wrong if it increases pain. The calculation could be made quite simply by taking each person affected by the action as one and adding up the numbers. If more are made happy than sad, the action is right. If more are made sad than happy, the action is wrong.

Goal-based morality, or following Bentham, utilitarianism, is morally serious. First, everyone counting as one has a radical equality. For the goal-based thinker, the child in sub-Saharan Africa counts as one, and the Prime Minister of Britain and one's own offspring each count as one, equally. Second, to consider the goal of an action is to consider that which motivates the action: if we did not seek certain outcomes, we would not act at all. In the context of medical research, for example, it is the desire for a cure for dementia, arthritis or cancer that produces the research proposals. In the context of policy-making and legislating, it may be the common good, economic growth, justice, choice or a healthy environment. There will be overarching goals, like 'the common good' or 'a cure for cancer', and then specific, targeted goals for a specific policy, piece of legislation or research project, such as 'establishing a national minimum wage' or 'testing the efficacy and effectiveness of tamoxifen'. These goals provide motivation and also parameters. People know what they are aiming at. It is a worthwhile, I would argue an essential, exercise to be absolutely clear about what one's goals are, whether in the field of policy-making, manifesto-writing, justice-delivering or any other field. What am I (really) trying to achieve here, and is it good?

But if we stop just at goal-based morality, as Bentham did, we soon run into difficulties. For we have nothing within goal-based morality to prevent us from performing actions that are not *intrinsically* good or right if they make more people happy than sad. Indeed, for strict goal-based thinkers, there is a moral requirement to perform those actions that increase happiness, whatever is involved. Moreover, for goal-based thinkers, there are no tragedies, because (assuming you can do the mathematics) there is always a right answer.

Take this slightly absurd example. A person, let us call her Jane, is healthy, with a full complement of functioning organs. Joe, however, is dying. He needs a heart transplant to save his life. Henry is also dying, in his case of lung disease. Corinne is dying of lung disease too. Helen and George are both dying of kidney disease. Rachel needs a liver to survive. Joe, Henry, Corinne, Helen, George and Rachel are all dying people, each one for want of an organ transplant. We need only kill Jane to save six lives. We are not distressed by this, if we are simply goal-based thinkers, because we know we are right to kill one in order to save six. And the fact that Jane is (say) a chief constable of police and Henry who needs a lung is a very wealthy businessman is not relevant, as whoever he or she is, each counts as one.

Except that we are distressed at the prospect, and not just, indeed not at all, because Jane is a chief constable. However wonderful and desirable saving six lives is, anyone who is not distressed by the thought of killing a healthy person in order to harvest his or her organs would be regarded as a sociopath at best. Just as, to take a real example, we would be regarded as heartless sociopaths not to be distressed by the people queuing at food banks, however much breaking benefit dependency may be an agreed goal. But within this wonderfully simple goal-based morality we have nothing to refer to to help us out of our plight. We have identified, and identify with, our good and desirable goal, and having counted the cost and found it weighs less in the balance, we are content to act. Goal-based morality is important, but not enough for the morally sensitive and courageous thinker.

Duty-based morality

Duty-based morality, by contrast, considers not the outcome of actions but their content, what is involved in their execution – Jane's execution, as it were. The duty-based moral thinker will ask, does my action conform with my moral principles? If it does, the action may be performed, whatever the consequences. If it does not, the action may *not* be performed, whatever the consequences. Such principles may include not harming and not lying. They may involve scriptural injunctions such as the Ten Commandments, or the Two Commandments to love God and neighbour or the Great Commandment found in all religions to treat others as you would wish yourself to be treated. These principles that tell us our duty are powerful moral guides to those who learnt them from a young age or strongly adhere to a law-based religious faith. Duty-based morality can, I suggest, also be defended on the grounds that some actions are 'simply wrong'. These may be understood as intuitive or faith-based reasons for being a duty-based moralist.

Immanuel Kant offers a reasoned justification for duty-based morality with his Categorical Imperative. The Categorical Imperative is rational, and it goes like this:

> Act according to a maxim which can at the same time make itself a universal law. Act only on that maxim whereby you can at the same time will that it would become a universal law. (Kant 1985, p.49, first published 1785)

To take an example Kant himself uses: suppose I need a great deal of money and I know that Caroline has that amount of money. I also know that she will not give me her money unless I promise to pay her back. I know that I will not be able to pay her back. My proposed action is to make a lying promise in order to obtain the money from Caroline.

This fails the Categorical Imperative. The maxim of the proposed act is that it is all right to gain money by making lying promises. That cannot become a universal law, because if it did, everyone would be making lying promises and no one would lend anyone any money. Nor can I consistently will that it should become a universal law, because Caroline would know that I was lying, and she would not lend me her money.

There is another foundation for duty-based morality, called natural law ethics, in which I discover the right way to behave from observing what is natural to me. Thomas Aquinas argued that it is right for a man and a woman to stay together for life because 'there is in men a certain natural solicitude to know their offspring' (Aquinas 1975, p.147), and if the relationship were broken and other sexual relations engaged in, no man would know which child was his. From the 'is' of a man's solicitude to know his offspring comes the 'ought' of a man and a woman staying together for life. This approach is dubious: it only works if we can agree what 'is', that is to say, what we mean by natural. If we think homosexual activity is unnatural, by natural law ethics it is also, and because of that, wrong. Some have argued as much.

Some moral philosophers argue that this weakness destroys the basis for natural law ethics altogether, but I would propose, rather, that our growing understanding of physiology and psychology, among other disciplines, requires us to rethink our natural law ethics. Just as, in ecological ethics, we understand better the natural rhythms of the soil and the weather and adjust our farming techniques accordingly, or ignore them at our peril, so we should adjust our treatment of each other as we understand each other better, in some cases without hesitation given prior outrageous behaviour due to lack of understanding and knowledge.

But even if we do not believe that we can derive an 'ought' from an 'is' (and libraries of books have been written demonstrating that it cannot be done), I think it is uncontroversial to assert that a professional role brings with it moral responsibilities: for example, the 'is' of being a doctor brings with it the 'ought' of having – always – a duty of care to one's patients. The 'is' of being a teacher brings with it the 'ought' of pedagogy and example to one's students. Similarly, the 'is' of taking up public office brings with it the 'ought' of selfless decision-making and moral rectitude articulated, *inter alia*, in the Nolan principles of selflessness, integrity, objectivity, accountability, openness, honesty and leadership (Committee on Standards in Public Life 1995). They come with the territory. They are duty-based moral requirements.

Duty-based morality is a much-needed counter balance to goal-based morality that does not know how to explain why killing Jane to harvest her organs is wrong. We need to be clear about the goals of a proposed action, and we then need to consider what is involved in executing the action. What will I, the moral agent, have to do in order to achieve that goal? Is it morally justifiable or not? Not to ask 'do the ends justify the means' but simply, regardless of the ends, are the means acceptable?

Let us imagine, for a moment, a Kantian, duty-based world – one where no one lied to anyone else, under any circumstances. I ask you what you think of my essay style, and you answer truthfully. You ask me what I think of your policy proposal (and let us say you are the minister and I am a civil servant in your department) and I answer truthfully. And remember, in this thought experiment, that you and I both know, *for certain*, that the other is telling the truth. So the praise as well as the criticism can be believed, without exception. What an extraordinary world that would be. We could, in this extraordinary world we are imagining, trust each other completely.

Even if it is possible to imagine such a world, would it be desirable, though? Kant famously, and worryingly, stated that since lying failed the Categorical Imperative and was always wrong, it was the case that even if a murderer chasing his victim asked you if the victim went 'that way' and you knew, you should tell the truth (Kant 2012, first published 1797).

Duty-based morality can easily tip into paternalism. For example, if I am a doctor, I might think that I know what my duty is towards my patient and be very certain what is right for him or her. What he thinks is irrelevant. Similarly, if I am a policy-maker, I might think I know what my duty in respect of a given policy might be, regardless of the views of those who will be affected by it. My moral certainty about how I should behave is not necessarily going to be the best thing for you. I secure my place in heaven, as it were, believing that I have done the right thing, never mind what you think or want.

Right-based morality

Right-based morality, our third moral approach, counters this paternalism. I am understanding 'right-based morality' specifically as the right to express one's autonomy. The focus is on those most affected by one's action, the stakeholders. In right-based thinking, it is their views, rather than an overall goal or one's own sense of moral rightness, that determine the action. In the medical profession, and in society more broadly, right-based morality has come to take precedence. In short, we have replaced responsibilities with rights: my action is ethical because it respects your autonomous choice rather than expresses my responsibility.

In the context of healthcare ethics and law, Ian Kennedy (1980) was an articulate defender of patient autonomy, arguing that between the doctor and the patient there is an imbalance of power that the law has to rectify by giving the patient the right of refusal to treatment, such that regardless of what the doctor thinks the patient needs, if the patient does not consent, any further treatment would be battery, that is, unlawful. Immanuel Kant suggested a characteristically robust basis for this, coining the moral precept 'so act always as to treat the other as an end in himself, and never merely as a means withal' (Kant 1985, pp.56–7, first published 1785). Thus the doctor's duty of care – always and everywhere applicable – is countered by a patient's autonomous disagreement. In right-based morality (and the law), the patient's view is the one that holds sway.

In the sphere of elected public office, there is a wrenching right-based test every five years as those who are ruled have the opportunity to let those who rule them know whether they want them to continue to have such power, and the decision of the ruled, the electorate, of course, is final. Referenda give right-based morality pride of place. Those public servants less close to the people affected by the consequences of their policy-making should nevertheless seek to know how they are affected and how they feel about it.

Important as right-based morality is, as with the other two approaches, on its own it is not enough. Strictly applied, if Philip were to give Anne a knife and ask her to kill him, because he really wants her to, and he is competent and knows the consequences of what he is asking, that would be sufficient right-based moral justification for Anne to kill him, because she is not to tell Philip what is rational or right behaviour, and he does not have to refer to any inner moral code, nor indeed to whether the consequences of such an action are more widely desirable. It is Philip's autonomy that Anne is respecting. Such thinking can be found in some of the arguments around euthanasia.

Right-based arguments are important, but they are not enough. For those in public office, seeking to please the public rather than lead or govern wisely has complicated and unsatisfactory consequences for everyone concerned. But the views of stakeholders matter, and not only because it is our duty to take them into account. It is the stakeholder's right to be heard that is the moral imperative here. Thus right-based thinking rounds off the other two approaches: once we have established the goal of our action, and determined what we have to do in order to achieve it, we should consult those most affected by the action without assuming their consent, however good we believe our proposed action may be.

Summary

I have offered three different ways of considering the morality of a proposed action: goal-based, which judges the rightness of the outcome of the action; duty-based, which judges the rightness of the action itself, regardless of outcomes; and right-based, which judges the action according to the wishes of those most affected by it. I have suggested that each of these approaches has strengths and weaknesses, and each has a place in our moral thinking. A thoughtful moral agent will take all three approaches into account when considering how to act. Like a three-legged stool, between them they provide stability, even on rocky ground.

Applications

The subtle art of policy-making can be helped by this analysis. The two examples I look at here are of necessity simplified but should show how the framework helps disentangle the different moral questions that need to be attended to. The first example is from the Department for Environment, Food and Rural Affairs (Defra) (flood defences) and the other is from the Home Office (border controls). First, Defra. A flood defence scheme is proposed that will protect thousands of households from flooding for the foreseeable future. A few hundred households will lose their homes to the scheme, and some habitats of non-human creatures will also be destroyed. One of the households belongs to the Prime Minister. From a goal-based perspective, the proposal is not just acceptable, it is morally obligatory, because more people will benefit than will be harmed. That one of the households belongs to the Prime Minister is irrelevant. From a Benthamite perspective, the non-human creatures do not figure in the calculation. From a duty-based perspective, that even one household (anyone's, not just the Prime Minister's) will be adversely affected is enough to give pause for thought, and so would the threat to non-human species and their habitats. The duty-based perspective will defend the intrinsic rather than utilitarian value of certain things and withstand the zeal of the utilitarian's moral purpose. Duty-based morality is more complicated, because people will not always, perhaps not often, agree on which moral principles have so much importance they trump the goal-based conclusions, but the perspective is an essential part of the moral consideration, precisely because it acknowledges incommensurables, literally priceless things. Sometimes the policy proposal requires the sacrifice of such important values or things that it should be resisted, whatever the consequences. Sometimes the duty-based perspective has to compromise and the goal-based perspective make concessions. What is not honest is to try to justify actions that are wrong in themselves by making them disappear in the utilitarian calculation. Even one affected household, whether or not it is the Prime Minister's, or one species' habitat harmed by the flood defence, is wrong: the harm is not removed because others benefit. Goal-based morality tempered by duty-based morality means that we face up to the true cost of our policies and means that we will, at the very least, seek to ameliorate those costs as the policy is developed.

Suppose it were possible to plan a flood defence scheme that harmed no household and destroyed no natural habitat and so fulfilled not only goal-based requirements but duty-based requirements as well. The people most affected by the flood defence scheme may still not want it to happen: they may have their reasons that are unknown to the policy-makers. Rather like a doctor prescribing a treatment to a patient without seeking his or her consent: however much the doctor might think the proposed action is in the patient's best interests, only the patient can really know, so a good doctor will always seek consent. It would be wrong to create a flood defence scheme without the consent of the stakeholders, and attending to this aspect of the policy is ensured by the right-based perspective. It may be the case that the wishes of the stakeholders have to be overridden, because the judgement is made that the goal-based and duty-based requirements outweigh the right-based ones. But that does not make it right. Honesty demands the acknowledgement that there was some moral failure, even if it was necessary.

Second, the Home Office. A tough border control is proposed. The goal is that serious harm to potentially large numbers of people will be averted. The cost will be long queues and aggressive interrogation that could irritate everyone and significantly harm a few. The numbers irritated or even harmed are minuscule when contrasted with the loss of human life that a terrorist attack threatens to bring about. However irritating or upsetting, a tough border control does not threaten death. The goal-based arguments are powerful. But the harm to some, such as a person being falsely accused of being a threat to the country or taken ill because of the wait, is morally problematic for the duty-based thinker. Even one frightened person harmed by detainment and interrogation or one dehydrated child waiting for hours in a hot car is wrong. The harm is not removed because others benefit. Goal-based morality tempered by duty-based morality means that the true cost of the policy proposal is acknowledged and taken seriously enough for amelioration to be part of the policy development.

Let us suppose that it is possible to plan a border control that was so well staffed by skilful and compassionate people, there were no queues, no mistaken detainments and no aggressive behaviour: such a scheme would fulfil not only goal-based requirements but duty-based requirements as well. But suppose the nation as a whole, or the majority in it, wanted free movement of people and wanted to accept the risk that attended upon such freedom? This might seem preposterous to the Home Office policy-makers. So do some refusals of treatment seem preposterous to some doctors. The right-based moral perspective recognizes that only the patient, only the public, can know what they want. Such knowledge is attendant upon proper information communicated well, and serious attention to this aspect of policy development will be paid if the right-based perspective is part of the approach. Again, right-based considerations may be outweighed by goal- or duty-based considerations. We should be fully aware that this is the case and recognize the moral cost. From a prudential point of view, ignoring the wishes of the people can have disastrous consequences over time, particularly if it seems to the people that their wishes have been repeatedly and consistently ignored.

The three-legged approach can help identify the moral questions other areas of public service pose. For the armed forces, goal-based concerns include questions such as whether their role is to protect British interests or secure international peace. Duty-based concerns include the cost of conflict to local communities, to armed forces personnel and to reputation both of government and the armed forces themselves. Right-based questions relate to local populations and governments of other countries where the Forces are based and, controversially, service personnel themselves.

An example in the context of the law of how the different approaches apply can be found in the case (Aintree v James 2013) that came to the Supreme Court about the withdrawing of life-sustaining treatment from a very sick patient whose family was contesting a previous judgment that had allowed this. Right-based concerns for the patient's autonomy were strenuously considered: though the patient was himself unable to express any wish, the court spent time considering what he might have wanted were he able to. Despite the need for a great deal of interpretation, the Mental Capacity Act (HMSO 2005) is to be applauded for its intention to recognize, even retrospectively, the wishes of individuals. The court spent time considering the wishes and views of his family as well as of the patient. It pondered the duty-based question of the inherent value, named as the sanctity, of life. The goal-based issue of resource allocation did not feature – a measure, perhaps, of the independence of the judiciary. The practice of the law upholding the right of individuals to a fair trial stands in firm opposition to goal-based arguments that will make statistics out of people. Rather, the goal-based moral issue was that justice must be done and be seen to be done.

The law enacts what the legislature lays down in the statute book. Opposite the Supreme Court on Parliament Square stands Parliament itself. For those tasked with making the law, goal-based questions are: what is this legislation trying to achieve? Is it to pacify hurt stakeholders? Is it to criminalize newly discovered unacceptable behaviour? Is it to regulate or de-regulate new or old practices? Duty-based questions include: will any group be harmed by the legislation? Can the harm be anticipated and clauses added to prevent it? Does that increase the bill's complexity to the point where it becomes impossible to implement? Right-based questions include whether the bill is what those most affected by it would want. William Temple (1956, pp.102–3) brought together goal- and right-based approaches when he suggested that:

> The art of Government is not to devise what would be the best system for saints to work, but to secure that the lower motives actually found among men prompt that conduct which the higher motives demand…the cause of justice and fellowship.

Conclusion: proper moral analysis is courageous

The three-legged stool, each leg of which represents one of the three approaches of goal-based, duty-based and right-based morality, stands firm even on rocky ground. Each leg needs to be the same length as the other. This does not mean that every decision favours each approach equally: as we have seen, this is well-nigh impossible. What it means is that each approach is given equal weight in consideration, and if one has to take precedence over the other, the cost is recognized. This intellectual squaring up to the moral cost of our decisions is courageous. When we see clearly and face up to the moral imperatives at stake in any decision, and do not back away when they conflict, we are showing moral courage. We are showing moral courage when we hold in our minds two conflicting statements that are nevertheless both true, or important, such as 'we must protect the land upon which we all depend' and 'people's homes must not flood'; or 'we must protect our citizens from terrorism' and 'people on harmless business must freely move'; or 'people must be allowed to die and to die well' and 'the intrinsic value of human life must be protected'. We are morally courageous when we wait with the paradox, because it makes our understanding grow to hold two conflicting but true statements together and makes possible a new solution not hitherto imagined because our understanding was not yet able to encompass it. Moral courage is waiting, looking, thinking, judging, clarifying, reconfiguring and, sometimes, coming up with a solution that allows all moral imperatives to be met, or, if a time-bound decision has to be made and no magical solution has presented itself, making a compromised decision but knowing and honestly admitting that that is what one has done and knowing exactly what has been compromised for the decision to be taken. Moral courage is, sometimes, concluding that one should do nothing.

MORAL PERCEPTION

Introduction

I have argued for the importance of taking different moral approaches into account when making moral decisions. That approach, rigorous and comprehensive as it may be, nevertheless requires something in addition, something prior: that is, the disposition to make moral decisions. We may be willing to drink the water of moral thinking, but what brought us to the water's edge in the first place? This essay will argue that the way we perceive the world and consequently feel about it is the determining factor in becoming a morally sentient, sensitive and courageous being. It will conclude that love, born of perceiving aright, is the ultimate and best moral disposition.

The argument is predicated upon a premise that does not go uncontested, particularly in the public square. This is that we all perceive from somewhere in particular: we all have a unique point of view. We stand, embodied beings, in a specific place that no one else can occupy; and who we are, which has been determined by a myriad of different influences, determines what and how we see. I am going to argue that we have this unique perspective, that it is porous to influence and that we therefore need to attend to those influences to ensure that the perspective we have is as well oriented towards goodness and truth (and beauty) as it can be. But first I have to address this objection. Public discourse, at its best, wants to be free of personal interest. In the nineteenth century, Gladstone strove to make the governing classes virtuous, articulating the need for a public space into which no private interest might intrude (Oborne 2007, p.xii). I think that in an honest attempt to meet that high requirement, public discourse has believed that it must take place in a vacuum from which the oxygen of belief, idea and prejudice has been banished. We who engage in public debate should seek to do so with a pure kind of rationality, taking up the three approaches framework (or other rational method of working out what is the right thing to do) in what Lord Sumption, speaking at a seminar at Westminster Abbey Institute, called 'a basic place' and applying it without fear or favour. The application of the three approaches framework without fear or favour is right and commendable. But no matter how hard we try, we cannot place ourselves 'nowhere'. We cannot help but bring what or whom we are to the moral table – including the disposition to come to the moral table in the first place. We are embodied and have myriad experiences and interactions from before birth till now that press upon us; we are influenced by the company we keep; we are limited: we cannot see beyond our own horizons of time and space and we have failings, all of us; we have obligations to those who depend upon us and those who have supported us; and we believe things, sometimes, secretly, really quite strange things.

In order to honour Gladstone's high requirement, rather than pretend we can leave these myriad influences at the edge of the public square, we should get to know them, declare them without proselytizing, recognize their uniqueness to us and attend to their good health, which means never being complacent about them. Good health is much dependent upon good company. The people we spend time with and the beliefs we entertain should challenge us to keep looking beyond our own horizons or at the very least recognize that the horizons have something beyond them that we cannot see and that we interrogate our beliefs to see the effect they have on our behaviour towards others who may not be at all like us. The choice of what company to keep can be made by noticing its effect. If it closes me down, hardens my arteries or makes me unjustifiably angry, defensive, fearful or weary, it is probably not good company. If it gives me energy, enjoyment, openness to everything and a willingness to serve others, it is probably good company.

The dispositions offered in what is to follow might be judged good company. When I came across them myself, they had the effect of shifting my perspective in such a way that I felt a profound connection with others and the planet. That feeling translated into love, and my behaviour towards others and the planet changed as a matter of course or consequence. I wanted to do the right thing by my neighbour, and I also gained a sense of context for my moral decision-making. The perceptions gave me a reason for wanting to engage in public discourse as disinterestedly, in the Gladstonian sense, as I could and to sustain my engagement even when the dilemmas were intractable and other people difficult to work with. I want, then, to show that how we feel towards something makes all the difference in the world to the way we treat it.

The four dispositions are: the interdependence of everything with everything else; the intrinsic value of everything; the existence and importance of sabbath; and the proper role of humanity. I have given them my own interpretation, but they were originally inspired by a short paper on ecological concern prepared for a Conference of the Anglican Communion over 20 years ago (Lambeth 1998, pp.86–92).

Interdependence

Hildegard of Bingen, a thirteenth-century doctor of the church, said, 'God has made all things in creation in consideration of everything else' (quoted in Fox 2000). Imagine the universe as a three-dimensional spider's web. All the threads are connected, closely or distantly, to all the other threads. Their strength and survival comes from their connectedness to the other threads. If a thread is cut in one place, or in just a few places, the web survives. But if too many threads are cut at once, not only do they collapse, but the whole web collapses. The evolutionary biologist E. O. Wilson wrote of the extraordinary riot of biological diversity that makes up the complex ecosystems upon which all life depends.

> Pull out [a] flower from its crannied retreat, shake the soil from the roots into [your] cupped hand, magnify it for close examination. The black earth is alive with a riot of algae, fungi, nematodes, mites, springtails, enchytraeid worms, thousands of species of bacteria. The handful may be only a tiny fragment of one ecosystem, but because of the genetic codes of its residents it holds more order than can be found on the surface of all the planets combined. It is a sample of the living force that runs the earth. (Wilson 2001, p.328)

It is diversity that makes all life possible: not just this or that species but the glorious extensive mix. Just as a diversity of species is needed to maintain life on the planet in response to various batterings, so a diversity of human responses is also needed to ensure the health of human communities. Cultural diversity is conducive to health and survival, mono-culture to disease and withering. As with a field whose soil goes sterile if the same crop is planted year after year, so with a community that never refreshes itself with the welcome addition of the stranger.

James Lovelock argued for a way of perceiving the earth in his Gaia hypothesis, in which we imagine the earth, including humans, as a single living entity, with all its parts dependent upon each other. Although we see and experience the different parts of the earth, and certainly ourselves, as separate from each other, we can shift our perception by analogy. Our own body is made up of many parts: the head, torso, arms and legs; hair, eyelashes, fingernails and toenails; skin; muscle and flesh under the skin, tendons, ligaments and the skeleton to give structure; organs and the fatty substance around them to protect them. All of these parts go together to make up a whole, and each part, while it has its distinct identity, is nevertheless profoundly connected to each other part, and 'body' is the word of which these interconnected parts are, together, the referent. Now think of the earth as a body. I draw on the writing of J. R. McNeill (2000) for the following description. Think of the *atmosphere* around the earth, at its outer edge receiving and reflecting the all-important sun's rays; at its lowest altitudes exchanging heat, moisture and gases with soil, water and living things. Think now of the *pedosphere*, the soil that lies on the outer crust of the earth, like skin on flesh, about half a metre thick, made of sand, clay, silt and organic matter, acting as a cleansing and protecting membrane between the lithosphere and the atmosphere. Now picture the *lithosphere*, the outer crust of the earth, which is about 120 kilometres thick, rock floating on molten rock. On average the earth's rocks have eroded, deposited on ocean floors as sediment, consolidated into rock again and been thrust up above sea level again 25 times in the history of the earth. Think of the *hydrosphere*, the plumbing of this blue planet that, like our own bodies, is mostly water. Water flows in the rainfall, in rivers and oceans, in watersheds, in our drinking, our washing and our tears. And finally, the *biosphere*, the sum of all the habitats in which species live, including every home in every part of the world, from the bubbling sea floor vents teeming with bacteria to glaciers at dizzy heights where the occasional beetle may be found and everything in between. Images from outer space show us the exquisite beauty of this single entity. Once one has begun to think in this way, seeing the undeniable dependence of everything upon everything else, it becomes harder to see our relationships with each other and the rest of the planet as transactional, between more or less inert beings, controlling or being controlled.

It is one thing to think of interdependence in theory; another to know it in practice. Evelyn Underhill, a twentieth-century mystic, wrote this exercise in her book *Practical Mysticism* to bring about a fundamental change in how we see, and we can try it as we read:

> Stretch out by a distinct act of loving will towards one of the myriad manifestations of life that surround you: and which, in an ordinary way, you hardly notice unless you happen to need them. Pour yourself out towards it, do not draw its image towards you... As to the object of contemplation, it

matters little. From Alp to insect, anything will do, provided that your attitude be right: for all things in this world towards which you are stretching out are linked together, and one truly apprehended will be the gateway to the rest... A subtle interpenetration of your spirit with the spirit of those 'unseen existences' now so deeply and thrillingly felt by you, will take place. Old barriers will vanish: and you will become aware that St Francis was accurate as well as charming when he spoke of Brother Wind and Sister Water. (Underhill 2000, pp.48–9, first published 1914)

The realization of interdependence not only means that we can see how everything is affected by everything else, but also that we have our place within the interweaving dance. Mary Oliver's poem 'Wild Geese' conveys this:

> Whoever you are, no matter how lonely,
> the world offers itself to your imagination,
> [...]
> over and over announcing your place
> in the family of things. (Oliver 1986)

Intrinsic value

Things have intrinsic value, not contingent value. They should be valued because they are, not because they can be used. To perceive this is to experience what Martin Buber described as a shift from regarding everything as *It* to regarding it as *Thou*, bringing it into relationship with oneself and thus into the deep understanding of our interdependence. In the Christian tradition we would say that God sees and loves every part, every minute movement of creation, and so we too cannot simply dismiss any part, or any one, as 'other'. There is nowhere called *away* where we can throw things, none we can call *other* to treat merely as a means to our own ends.

Such an appreciation of the whole of creation as sacred stands in contrast to the technological mindset described by Martin Heidegger (1977) and, more recently, Pope Francis (2015) in which everything and everyone, including ourselves, has value only when it comes into use. When not in use, it simply stands in reserve, waiting to be used. It has no intrinsic value. A Victorian explorer, a clergyman, expressed astonishment at discovering an exquisite orchid deep in the heart of the rainforest where no human, so far as he knew, had ever penetrated. Why on earth had God put it there?

There has never been anyone like you, reader, before, and there will never be anyone like you ever again. You are and always will be unique. The same is true of every blade of grass. E. O. Wilson (2001) contends that we should value species as much as we value works of art because they are both kinds of miracles, born of a long, long history of development and struggle against the odds. Moreover, it is a shared history. Humans evolved along with everything else. Humans are not temporary tenants on an earth that is simply a backdrop for our merely human dramas or a bottomless larder of good things to plunder. We did not land here from elsewhere and adapt. The rocks and we are as we are because we evolved together, which explains why, for most of us, the natural world is experienced as restorative.

Undoing the technological mindset and recognizing our shared intrinsic value is addressing a kind of addiction, one that, in John Zizioulas' words, has us seeking to 'pass everything through our hands' (Zizioulas 1990, p.4). It is a mindset perhaps created, certainly expressed most clearly, by René Descartes, whose 'I think therefore I am' asserted an identity of a self that was separate from matter and could dominate it. The 'cogito self' could become 'master and possessor of nature' (Descartes 1970, first published 1637). Out of such an attitude came the Industrial Revolution with its attendant goods and also, we now know, harms. Without a profound re-orientation of our perceptions away from the idea that the earth is a tool for human use and towards a realization of our interdependence and our intrinsic value, we will not find any lasting solution to the ecological crisis we now face; not just ecological, but social as well. The concepts of interdependence and intrinsic value move us away from differentiating between the good of our bit of humanity and any other bit, or between humanity and the good of the planet, a view that entails prioritizing humanity when they compete, sawing off the branch we are sitting on, as it were, because we need fuel.

Simone Weil writes of prayer in a way that can help undo the habitual separation, transaction and control of each other that is the habit of our age. Prayer, Weil said, was attention, and attention:

> ...consists of suspending our thought, leaving it detached... and ready to be penetrated by the object... Above all our thought should be empty, waiting, not seeking anything, but ready to receive in its naked truth the object that is to penetrate it... The love of our neighbour in all its fullness simply means being able to say to him: 'What are you going through?'... This way of looking is first of all attentive. The soul empties itself of all its own contents in order to receive into itself the being it is looking at, just as he is, in all his truth. (Weil 2001, p.62)

Sabbath

It is salutary to note that in the creation myth of Genesis, the crown of creation is not humanity, formed on the sixth day, but the sabbath, the seventh day, in which even God has a rest, and we do not imagine He did so because He was tired. The prayer that is attentive also calls us to stillness and silence. All traditions offer their times of prayer, contemplation, meditation, withdrawal and abstinence from doing and achieving. The Hebrew scriptures include land and neighbour in this rest, with the requirement every seven years to leave land fallow and every 50 years to forgive all debts and return all goods, a jubilee call to stop and take stock. Sabbath is not merely a pause for breath between bouts of doing, achieving and consuming, but a deep dive into peace for its own sake. The rest is literally that, restorative. In his poem 'Shadows' D. H. Lawrence wrote 'I have been dipped again in God and new-created' (Lawrence 1994). Restoration implies atonement, which is the sense the Hebrew scriptures give it. Stopping the rush can make possible appropriate penitence for unintended harm.

Some of us view the idea of sabbath with terror. If we have attached value only to our achievements and not to ourselves, then stopping achieving robs us of our value, and we become pointless to ourselves. Only that is not what happens, because, we discover, the feeling of pointlessness grows, not in the quiet, but in the rush, as we run away from our terrible fear of death. As Pablo Neruda wrote in his poem 'Keeping Quiet':

> If we were not so single-minded
> about keeping our lives moving
> and for once could do nothing,

perhaps a huge silence
might interrupt this sadness
of never understanding ourselves
and of threatening ourselves with death.

(Neruda 1979)

Try this: accept the gift of a 'little sabbath' next time you are holding your hands under a slow dryer in a public lavatory, being held up in a queue or waiting for a train. Instead of rushing out of the door with wet hands, or reaching for your phone to check for messages, just wait and take a few deep breaths. It will begin to accustom you to the idea of stopping and possibly make you readier for longer sabbaths. And try this: calculate your journey times with generosity, and ten minutes before it is time to leave, start to get ready. Your journeys will be transformed. You are not in a hurry, so you will enjoy the journey and you will notice and appreciate the things and people you meet on the way. (When I am late, I turn into a monster. Things and people I meet are no longer of intrinsic interest, they are simply infuriating obstacles.) Evelyn Underhill offers an analogy using the shape of the cross in which the horizontal bar represents the journey through life and the vertical bar the present moment, always now, deeply now, in this place. Every footfall is now, and with such a perception every footfall can be felt as being on sacred ground.

Which comes first, the perception that things are of intrinsic value and interdependent, which slows us down because we cannot claim that our achievements are of greater importance, or slowing down and taking time to look as Evelyn Underhill would have us, and thus seeing intrinsic value and interdependence? They come together.

There is no manual for changing perceptions. We just have to agree that it is possible and then take every opportunity to look, or slow down, whichever occurs to us first. The greatest rest of all is that which follows meaningful work, to which, we might argue, every human has the right. We are tormented by an economy that forces humans to do violence to their souls by conforming to utilitarian demands for greater productivity serving economic growth that, in turn, serves only itself. For those who cannot keep up with the fast-paced, knowledge-based demand, there is no work. Rest is no rest for them, because it is enforced and has no end. For those who can and do keep up, rest is denied because the demands come home with them in the powerful connecting tool of their phones. For those who enjoy the fruits of the economy that serves growth only, without contributing their own labours, the rest is as meaningless as that of the forcibly unemployed, only more comfortable. Why not envision an economy that serves the human need for meaningful work? What has made intelligent humanity fall into the exhausting trap of economic slavery?

The role of humanity

In *Straw Dogs*, John Gray (2003) lambasts Christianity and then humanism for giving humans the notion that we are special, pointing out all the ecological trouble that has caused. He suggests that our greatest gift to the universe, the part we should be playing given all our talents and abilities, is 'simply to see'. James Lovelock agrees. In his account of the earth as Gaia, he points out that with the advent of the human species she, Gaia, has at last been able to hold up a mirror to her face and see her own beauty – in the astonishing images we have of the earth from outer space. Humans, in James Lovelock's account, are the brain of Gaia. Simone Weil's prayerful attention, *not* action, is service. This was Dame Cicely Saunders' great insight into treatment at the end of life: when there was nothing to be done and a life was simply ebbing away, accompanying a person on that journey was the greatest service one could offer and indeed a great privilege to perform. When asked what he was doing in a place, a monk simply said, 'Keeping it' (Chryssavgis 2003, p.33).

Simply seeing is a good place to start but inevitably humans will move into action. Released from the compulsion to act in order to prove our worth, and working with a mindset that sees everything else as having intrinsic value, as *Thou* not *It*, we have the opportunity to act wisely. Here the three approaches of goal-based, duty-based and right-based analysis, described in the previous essay, can be employed as we consider the moral worth of our proposed actions, but with humility born of our awareness of our interdependence and the intrinsic value of the other. What is the good goal towards which our actions should be directed? Whose good is being promoted? What will we be required to do in order to achieve that goal? What of those affected by the action? Who are the stakeholders when 'God has made all things in creation in consideration of everything else'?

Conclusion: proper moral perception is emotionally courageous and also necessary

Four perceptions have been suggested: first, that everything is interdependent, woven into relationship such that every action affects every other part; second, that everything has intrinsic value, not for what it can achieve but for itself; third, that sabbath rest is available and matters; and fourth that humanity must act, it cannot just sit around and look, but should act from the love these perceptions evoke and with moral care.

Peter Hennessy, in his essay *Establishment and Meritocracy*, captures the weakness of the meritocratic ideal when he notices its potential price, 'creating a detached and self-regarding elite insensitive towards those who have not soared up meritocratic ladders of their own' (Hennessy 2014, p.60). Being clever is not enough. He quotes Richard Chartres, former Bishop of London, who said this:

> It is not difficult to see why we are so keen to widen our knowledge and why we are so little concerned to increase our capacity to love – knowledge translates directly into power; love translates into service. (Hennessy 2014, p.55)

The global challenges of the twenty-first century confound utilitarian solutions and do not recognize national boundaries. James Martin (2007) likens the century to a river that is flowing faster and faster towards a canyon caused by a combination of stresses: climate change, loss of biodiversity, acidification of oceans, terrorism and internecine wars, mass migration and population growth. The transition generation, living through this time, must pilot its way through the canyon such that the world into which we emerge is a compassionate, not a merciless dog-eat-dog, world. The moral courage needed to face these challenges needs to spring from a deep emotional sense of the importance of seeing the challenges holistically. We have to address the challenges but we cannot do so as Cartesian selves, thinking we are 'masters and possessors of nature'. Without yet knowing what that compassionate world might look like, nor yet knowing quite how we are to pilot our way through the canyon, we have to know that solutions must have these qualities: they must be inclusive of the whole human race and in tune with all of nature; these are interdependent and have intrinsic value. It takes moral courage to retain a commitment to these qualities and look for their presence in any policy decision or law that we make, to keep that global perspective even as we address the problem that is facing us today. We should bring all our talent, wisdom, love, enthusiasm, skill and science, not as godlike problem-solvers but with an attempt at atonement and restoration, so we leave things better than we found them, knowing more fully what 'better than' should look like and for whom. We are in love with our neighbour and we are aware that our 'neighbour' includes everyone and everything because we are connected to them. We are diligent in thinking clearly and acting decisively because we have emotional endurance born of an inspired and loving perspective.

The challenge is considerable. If you are responsible for public service of just one country, you may argue, it is quite big enough, and one's protection of interests has to stop there. That is self-evidently true of any national government: of course, its role is to look after the interests of the citizens of that country. But whom do we have, other than our national leaders, to be visionary? Institutions such as the UN depend upon national leaders agreeing to work together, and so we have a kind of international 'prisoners' dilemma'. (Two prisoners, A and B, interrogated separately, are both offered choices between testifying against the other or remaining silent. If A testifies against B and B remains silent, A will be let off and B will receive 10 years' imprisonment, and vice versa. If both A and B testify against each other, both will receive two years' imprisonment. If both remain silent, both will receive six months' imprisonment, the maximum sentence the court can give in the absence of evidence.) Everyone has to trust each other to do the right thing, or everyone suffers as each seeks only to serve his or her own country's self-interest. Iain McGilchrist (2009) recognized that looking to our Cartesian rationalist selves to solve such dilemmas will never solve them. We cannot calculate our way out of the canyon. We have to trust each other.

We have examples from the past of leaders who have not only transcended national self-interest but also, crucially, inspired their citizens to share their international vision. Jeffery Sachs (2013) has written about the speech that J. F. Kennedy made after the Cuban Missile Crisis, showing how he shifted from being on the brink of blowing up the planet in 1962 to helping to bring about the Test Ban Treaty of 1963. In the speech, J. F. Kennedy speaks of common humanity and human beings' moral responsibility for each other. He sets a vision beyond the fixed horizons of the US people and shows the way to get there, so the vision is not just motherhood and apple pie, and people are both morally uplifted and given hope because they see the path to that place they in their heart of hearts long to reach.

Such an example offers hope, in turn, that such vision can be offered and sustained through the difficult years ahead, because what we want and what will make us flourish is also what the planet needs. Because I am interdependent, porous to my neighbour, unable to hermetically seal myself off from him or her; because I am of intrinsic value, and so is he or she; because when I rest, I realize that my greatest happiness does not come from feeding voracious desire; because when I work, I want to work meaningfully, so as to earn and enjoy my rest: for all these reasons, who I am and what I do should be, without fuss, good for all. Then I can say, with St Augustine, 'Love, and what you will, do.'

MORAL PRACTICE

Introduction

A cockerel had been purchased by a farmer to service his hens. Full of bright promise and good intentions, the cockerel went into the hen coop to start his work – and found that he was incapable. He failed, miserably. The hens cackled at him and shooed him out of their nest. Flopping around the farmyard, distressed as anything, feeling useless and foolish, the cockerel found he was drawn despite himself to the field of cows where, without a shadow of a doubt, and clearly with great skill and enjoyment, the bull was performing the very service at which the cockerel had been so dreadfully lacking. The cockerel drooped miserably on the fence by the side of the field. The bull, having finished his day's work, sauntered over to the cockerel.

'What's up, old chap?' he asked.

'I've failed,' said the cockerel. 'I'm supposed to do to the hens what you've just been doing to the cows, and I've failed. I – I just can't seem to manage.'

The bull was sympathetic. 'I've a solution for you,' he said.

The cockerel brightened. 'Really?'

'It always works, believe me,' said the bull, with total conviction.

'Tell me, tell me,' said the cockerel eagerly. 'I'll do anything you say!'

'For the next three days,' said the bull, looking straight at the cockerel, 'nibble a bit from the edge of my droppings – you can choose the drier ones – just a bit, every day for three days. You should find that does the trick.'

The cockerel, though slightly disgusted, did as the bull recommended. For three days, he nibbled at the droppings. Nothing seemed to change, he felt as droopy and useless as ever, until the evening of the third day, when, as if by magic, he perked up. So much so that he went straight to the hen coop and, taking no nonsense from the hens, performed his duty on every one of them. It took till midnight. He was so thrilled at his success that he flew up to the highest point in the farmyard, the roof of the farmhouse, threw his head back and let out a triumphant and very loud 'cock-a-doodle-doo'.

The farmer, wakened violently from a deep sleep, leapt out of bed, reached for his gun, ran out of the front door and shot the cockerel, who died instantly.

And the moral of the story is: if you get to the top through bullshit, don't crow about it.

The story balances merit and gift, something Peter Hennessy discusses in his essay *Establishment and Meritocracy* (2014). Our achievements are a mixture of what we have worked for and deserved, and what we have been given. Born with wealth or title, we feel (or should feel) obliged to turn what we have been given without deserving into service of others. Born not with wealth or title but with brains and ambition, the obligation remains.

Storytelling

We remember stories when we forget a great deal else. Stories have an effect, and this essay will explore stories that inspire, stories that lie, stories that show how interdependent we are, stories we tell of ourselves and those that others tell of us. Stories describe pathways and impel us into action. J. F. Kennedy inspired US citizens to see beyond their national self-interest to the good of all and, argues Sachs (2013), showed the way to get there. Using storytelling, I will seek to describe a path from feeling and thinking morally to acting morally.

The material I am going to use draws substantially from Joseph Campbell's work, in particular his *The Hero with a Thousand Faces* (1968, first published 1949). He shows how in nearly every myth that has ever been recounted there is a common thread or plot in which the protagonist or hero embarks on a quest that transforms him or her and from which he or she returns with the elixir that in turn serves others.

This mono-myth describes the journey of the self into virtue and communitarian ethics. But there are two lenses I want to use, because of the particular circumstances of this essay, whose primary audience, like the lecture upon which it is based, is public servants. One is that the hero of the story, because it is us, and we are public servants, starts off knowing that this journey is not about me. The public servant acts, by virtue of his or her title, for others. That is what the Nolan principles of selflessness, integrity, objectivity, accountability, openness, honesty and leadership all point the public servant towards. Moreover, we can also think of the story as being about the development of the collective, the community, institution, nation or human family. Because we are public servants, we can let our minds work on the story in this non-individualistic way. The other lens I want to suggest is that rather than use the word 'hero', I will use the word 'pilgrim', removing the connotations of specialness that 'hero' implies and joining us with the countless anonymous pilgrims who have journeyed to Westminster Abbey over the centuries.

The pilgrim's journey

Think of your life, or that of your institution, as a film. You, unique you, like whom there never has been and never will be anyone, ever, are the protagonist of the film of *Life of [your name]*. What kind of a film has your life been so far? Romantic comedy? Tragedy? Thriller? And what kind of a protagonist have you been so far? Are you enjoying yourself? Are you challenged, or are you bored? Are you open to new possibilities? Do you know who or what you want to be? What sets your belly on fire? Do you feel as though you are treading a well-worn path through a thousand weary days of getting dressed and going to work, feeding the family, a slave to the quotidian calls on your time and your purse, with no clear idea of what you are doing or where you are going? Do you feel even more of a victim than that? Are you bullied? Are you physically or mentally challenged in some way that makes you feel you are being held back from doing what you have always wanted to do? What would you do if you were not afraid?

This is where the story begins; stage one: *The Ordinary World*. It is your platform, your comfort zone. In our

Fellows' programme, which uses this framework, I show film clips from *Gandhi*, a classic hero's journey, and this stage is illustrated by the beginning of the film, when Gandhi, a young attorney just moved to South Africa, is thrown out of his first-class carriage for being a 'coolie'. The indignity of his treatment is the Ordinary World of the majority of South Africans who are not white.

Something is calling the pilgrim out of this unsatisfactory Ordinary World; stage two: *Hearing the Call*. Gandhi is put upon his mettle: something must be done about injustice, and indeed he successfully defies the Pass Laws, winning an early victory against apartheid. He returns to India a hero, and is clearly expected to join the fight against the British for independence. This is his call. The call may come from inside you or outside. You may have heard such a call, a *vocation*, to public service. It is undeniable and often unwelcome.

And indeed, Gandhi turns the call down. He has to build up his attorney's practice, he protests. He has a family to feed now. Stage three of the journey is *Refusing the Call*. For any number of reasons, the call cannot be answered. It is an important stage: we have all had the experience perhaps of leaping too enthusiastically at a suggestion, rushing into action and falling flat on our faces. Refusing the call is the moment when you take stock and question the wisdom of the call. But it can also be the rearing up of fear and self-doubt. You are scared, faced with a step into the dark that you know will present difficulties you may not be able to deal with; you do not know if you have it in you; you do not know what is coming if you respond. It is a move out of your ordinary, safe, known, comfortable world.

But then, as you sit around in your now profoundly dissatisfied state, thinking of all the hundreds of reasons why you should not start and knowing they are sounding increasingly unconvincing, you meet someone who knows what you are capable of, believes in you and the vision of your journey, and knows how to help you take the first step. You *Meet your Mentor*, stage four in the journey. Gandhi's old teacher tells him he is capable of accepting the challenge. More, there is no one else who can do it, who can command the respect Gandhi can, who has been tested and not found wanting in South Africa. There are plenty of people with wealth who can support him. Only he can lead India to freedom from oppression. Critically, he is told what the first step is: to 'find India' – to travel across India and see what she is. Your mentor may be someone you only briefly meet; it may even be a book or a painting. Whatever or whomever it is, the mentor knows you have it in you to respond to the call and awakens a response in you. The mentor stands still, note. It is the protagonist or pilgrim who has to take the step forwards and the mentor cannot do that for him or her. Helicopter parenting and micro-managing fail because they do not set protagonists free to risk their own decisions and take responsibility for it. The mentor stands still like a signpost, doing no more than to point in the right direction and believe in the ability of the pilgrim to go there.

Thus stage five is passed: you *Cross the Threshold*. You make a commitment to the journey. This is a profound moment, a step into the dark. You have said yes to change without fully knowing what that will entail or whether you will be able to manage what it does entail. You have surrendered the safe control of your Ordinary World, cut the ties, left the known shore.

An excellent illustration of this stage of the journey can be found in the Council of Elrond scene in *The Lord of the Rings*. The hobbit Frodo has brought the ring as far as Rivendell, the kingdom of the elves, and Elrond, the king of the elves, has summoned all the 'goodies' together: the dwarves, the humans, the elves, Gandalf, Frodo. The ring sits in the middle of the gathering as the group ponders what to do. Elrond forestalls any notion that the power of the ring might be used against Sauron, the evil one. He knows, as by now does Frodo, that its power is itself evil and will change those who try to make it serve their purpose. Moreover, it is stronger than anyone present, which Gimli the dwarf discovers when he tries to smash the ring with his axe. Elrond declares that the ring must be destroyed, and the only way that is going to happen is if it is thrown back into the fire whence it was forged: the fire at the heart of Mordor. A row erupts: one does not simply walk into Mordor, guarded by a thousand armies of orcs. And who is going to have charge of the ring? The dwarves and elves do not trust each other; the humans are divided, and soon everyone is on his feet, shouting to be heard. We see Frodo looking at the ring and wincing at the noise, as if the ring is already working its evil power on those present, turning them against each other.

And then, in the midst of the row, Frodo stands up, and being a hobbit he is of course only half the height of anyone present except Gimli. He says, 'I will take the ring to Mordor.' At first no one hears him so he says it again and silence falls. 'I will take the ring to Mordor,' he says. 'But I do not know the way.' This is the moment that Frodo crosses the threshold onto his journey, stepping into darkness, knowing that he will be stretched beyond anything he can imagine and not knowing if he will make it through.

And then, one by one, each of the Council members declares his support. 'I will be your guide,' says Aragorn.

'You will have my bow,' says Legolas the elf. 'And my axe,' says Gimli. 'I will help you in any way I can,' says Gandalf. And then the three other hobbits emerge from the bushes determined not to be left out. And so the fellowship of the ring is formed, but only *after* the pilgrim has crossed the threshold. And that does seem to be the way the stories – our stories – go. The really worthwhile things are only attainable if we make a commitment to the journey towards them, and the help on the way only emerges after the commitment has been made. Note, the help is indispensable. The journey is about community, not individuality. Frodo could not have done it without the help of the fellowship, but he still had to show leadership in making the commitment as an act of trust and hope. The clip from the film *Gandhi* that we use for the Fellows shows him switch from refusing to join the violent revolutionaries to accepting the mantle of leadership, but the way in which it happens determines the nature – non-violent – of the leadership he will unwaveringly show. It is a subtle moment. A farmer who is a tenant of a British landlord mercilessly making him work the land to grow cash crops, not able to feed himself or his family, with even water supplies cut off in punishment for intransigence, walks the distance to the ashram where Gandhi has enclosed himself, spinning, not able to see clearly what he should do, if anything. The farmer sits and speaks. Gandhi listens. Then, gesturing to the man to eat the food placed before him, Gandhi turns and exchanges a long, steady look with his wife. In that moment, the conviction, strength and direction come to him, and everything changes.

Stage six, *Trials, Allies and Enemies*, is the journey itself beginning in earnest and this is where the pilgrim learns whom his or her allies are and whom the enemies are.

You face obstacles and learn which are unreal and of your own making, such as fear, and overcome them. You face trials, you make mistakes, you fall over, you get up, you realize that the journey is not about you at all but about everyone else: in other words, you grow in moral courage and discernment. The journey is changing you. For Gandhi, there are dissident voices to win over, particularly those who seek violent means to the goal of independence. There are eager young men longing to play their part who need meaningful tasks. There are those who will never be persuaded, and their power must be neutralized if it cannot be ignored. Staying power, focus, growing awareness, responsiveness, charm and the right kind of conviction are all imperative qualities for the pilgrim whose journey is unfolding before him or her.

In all the great stories and endeavours there comes a point on the journey when everything goes wrong. This is stage seven: *Facing the Darkness*. Your friends have deserted you, you have forgotten why you started on the journey, you are uncertain and afraid and everything that you thought you had learnt seems to have gone, along with your allies. The scene from *Gandhi* that we use to illustrate this stage is the harrowing slaughter by General Dyer of a large crowd of Indians gathered peacefully but illegally. Gandhi sees the price that his movement is asking of the people of India and his doubts and those of his followers nearly undo the whole enterprise.

If we have been through this story once or twice, we know – but only afterwards – that the darkest hour is just before the dawn. The absolute darkness is only an appearance because there is a bend in the tunnel and once you reach the corner you will see the light at the end. If you are going through hell, *keep going*.

The darkness fades, sometimes with the light breaking through. Sometimes it is because time simply passes. The darkness does not last if the pilgrim keeps moving forwards. Stage eight, *The Great Ordeal*, is nigh. This is the high point towards which the journey has been inexorably moving, the moment you have been being trained for in the testing stages of the journey, and everything in you is ready, even if it does not feel like it at the time: the speech, the giving birth, the match, the performance, the job interview, election day and so on.

This story, all the more powerful for the diffidence of his speech, comes from a former head of MI5:

I was put in mind [by the hero's journey narrative] of our collective leadership experience over 2005 to 6, with the 7/7 attacks and the 21/7 failed attacks. Paradoxically, the high point was not 7/7 but 21/7. Coming two weeks to the day after 7/7, we were already tired, and 21/7 made us fear that there was a whole series of these attacks already planned and of which we knew nothing, on top of which the 21/7 perpetrators had got away and could have another go. That was a really terrifying thought, institutionally and personally. Of course, all you can do is take a deep breath, press on and trust that by doing your jobs well and applying what you have learnt, you will turn the corner. In a sense we did, with the discovery of the 21/7 attackers' hideout in West London (remember the photos of the man on the balcony in his boxers?). That wasn't the end of it, and that autumn was tough, with wave after wave of credible intelligence of terrorist plotting against the UK. In October, we got to a point where we started to worry that we would be unable to respond to any new reporting. Again, we kept plugging away, and finally with the disruption of the liquid bomb plot (and other less well-remembered operations that summer of 2006) we seemed to have gained the initiative and to be able to breathe again. That wasn't the end of the struggle, but it did seem we had turned a corner and achieved some breathing space... (Jonathan Evans, personal communication)

The Great Ordeal is not necessarily a big, exciting moment but can be a gruelling test of endurance, skill and intelligence under pressure that does not let up. The MI5 officers just kept putting one pilgrim foot in front of another. In the film *Gandhi* the scene is shown where thousands of Indians walk towards the salt factory at Dharamsala and are violently rebuffed, wave after wave of them moving forwards without violence and without co-operation. The action is symbolic: the salt in the factory is from the Indian Ocean and its profits, therefore, should go to the Indians, not to the British. It is the deciding moment as the press report the terrible injuries inflicted on the unarmed and peaceful Indians and Britain loses not only her military authority but also her moral authority. Gandhi is invited to attend a conference in London to discuss the possible independence of India, at last. Importantly, we notice that Gandhi is in prison at the time of the action on the salt factory. The story is now owned by the Indians themselves; it is no longer about him.

The ninth stage is *Claiming the Prize*. For the public servant or pilgrim hero the prize that is only for him or her is not the real prize, whether it is the trophy, the election, the vote in Parliament or being the one to ensure the bomb plot fails.

Baroness D'Souza told this story:

I was in what we thought of as post-Taliban Afghanistan in early 2002 – a still traumatized country reeling from the

Soviet occupation, the civil war and the reign of terror by the Taliban. I came across a small bundle of energy and goodness called Aziz Royesh who had started a school for girls in a half-ruined hut teaching about 30 children in three shifts. To cut a long, long story short I was so impressed by him and what he aimed to do (a man who had been educated at a Red Cross primary school when he was a refugee in Pakistan) that I began to raise funds – in really small amounts – for him. Over the years, the school (Marefat High School) has flourished and become what has been called the St Paul's of Kabul – with 3000 students, half of whom are girls, and over 95% of whom go on to higher university education all over the world...but who return to teach at the mother school. It is an outstanding success driven by this man and is providing cohorts of young people who are Afghanistan's future leaders and who are versed in the liberal arts including ethics, civic duties, human rights and languages as well as the sciences. (Baroness D'Souza, personal communication)

Frances had to stop visiting when she became Lord Speaker, for security reasons, but to her delight her daughter became involved, a journalist who was, in her words 'at the rather frivolous end – *Vogue* and the like' (Baroness D'Souza, personal communication).

Frances' prizes were not for herself:

My joy at the development of the school is matched by witnessing the development of my daughter into the person she has become through a chance encounter with a society that is living and has always lived on the edge of brutality, war and extreme poverty. (Baroness D'Souza, personal communication)

The journey does not end with the prizes. There is a critical tenth stage, a *New Level of Life*, where, transformed by our journey individually or collectively, we stand ready to continue our lives' journeys as servant leaders, strong in ourselves, with moral courage and discernment thoroughly awakened and exercised. New journeys begin. For India, the new journey was one of establishing democracy but also, wrenchingly and damagingly, of Partition. The hero's journey myth is not a story with a happy ending, it is just a story in which we participate as interdependent players, often leaving the story before we know the ending or not knowing what the consequences of the ending might be.

This is the way to inspire ourselves and others, not only to feel and think morally, but also to act. The pilgrim's journey is a dynamic map. Most worthwhile endeavours follow a similar trajectory. Like J. F. Kennedy, we describe our noble vision, beyond the horizon of narrow self-interest, and we describe the path to that place where we all long, in our heart of hearts, to be, knowing the journey will not be easy because no worthwhile endeavour is.

Being human is not easy. None of our choices and actions is completely right: we are fallible people in a confusing world. Joseph Campbell said that life is like coming into a cinema in the middle of a film, not being allowed to ask anyone what is going on and leaving before the end. And still having to make decisions! Paul Ricoeur (1975, p.91) suggests we are all *in medias res*: one among many who have gone before us, are with us now or who will come after us. We play our part and make our contribution, never quite knowing the extent of its value. I have offered some structure but I know well that structures can only make limited sense of what is a bigger mystery than any of our brains can fathom. As Thomas

More said to his daughter Margaret in the play *A Man for all Seasons* (Bolt 1960):

> God made the angels to show Him splendour, as He made animals for innocence and plants for their simplicity. But Man He made to serve Him wittily, in the tangle of his mind.

The narratives of public servants

One of the prices those in public office pay is that others tell stories about you. They are caricatures, and they can be cruel. Here are stories about the public servants around Parliament Square, told and re-told by lazy minds not prepared to find out the truth.

The MPs are elected public servants with brittle egos, currying favour like celebrities, desperately seeking attention, motivated by ambition, bending like reeds in the wind that blows according to consumer preferences, having to seek and then retain power. They are greedy and, having been elected on merit, believe themselves to be entitled to privileges denied other citizens. The non-elected politicians of the Upper House are safe in their ermine, their titles bought through political donations and other favours, fatly claiming expenses for doing little. The judges take advantage of the low esteem in which politicians are held, drawing legislative power craftily into their web. The civil servants either exercise their own crafty 'Sir Humphry' influence behind the scenes or, threatened with creeping politicization, burrow down into their shrinking departments, turning away from the costly responsibility of speaking truth to power, feeling betrayed and victimized as their ministers brief against them and they cannot defend themselves publicly. The mischievous media tell the story that is 'too good to check'.

These are the stories that may be told about the public servant – *are* told about them. What are the stories they will tell of themselves? How will they ensure they are good and true? Here are some suggested alternative narratives to articulate and to aspire to:

Elected public servants who 'never lead the nation wrongly through love of power, desire to please, or unworthy ideals but laying aside all private interests and prejudices keep in mind their responsibility to seek to improve the condition of all mankind' (quoted from the prayers said daily in the chamber of the House of Commons). Members of the Upper House who live by and speak authentically from principle to set the tone of legislation, and who scrutinize, line by line, the bills that pass through their hands to ensure no devil comes to life in the detail. Judges who serve justice not bureaucracy, who administer justly the law of the land, debated and agreed by Parliament whose role is to decide what the law should be. Civil servants whose steady hand on the tiller holds fast the boat, flexible against the prevailing political winds and the choppy seas of 'events, dear boy, events', but not so flexible as to swing too far either side of the compass direction of 'the good' and writing a politician's name in the wake. Journalists who 'empower citizens with clear and relevant information, to nourish the national conversation with understanding', as BBC Home Editor Mark Easton put it (personal communication).

Conclusion: attend to the direction of travel, not the destination

These are, or should be, non-negotiables. But they are also ideals from which we all fall short. Hence I am so taken by the idea of the journey to goodness, rather than the Pelagian requirement to be good absolutely, actually a Christian heresy. It is a heresy to which MPs in particular, prodded by an unforgiving media, are prone: they cannot be allowed to learn goodness, changing over time, they must arrive, as it were, morally fully formed. But a journey without pitfalls and mistakes and challenges and scary moments is not just boring, it makes life meaningless. It is not really a journey at all.

I stand in profound respect of those who take up public office. I believe we should give them all our support. We need their strength – their moral strength. But we only deserve their moral strength if we provide the community out of which it can grow – where else do public servants come from if not from among us? – and so, in the end, strengthening moral courage in public life is a call to every one of us to take moral responsibility, to set our face towards the good and travel towards it, together.

Building Communities

A Conversation Between
Mary McAleese and John Hall

Introduction

This conversation between Professor Mary McAleese, former
President of the Republic of Ireland, and Dr John Hall,
Dean of Westminster, is based upon their public dialogue
in Westminster Abbey on the hundredth anniversary of the
1916 Easter Rising.

JOHN HALL

How does a Catholic from the North of Ireland come to be
President of the Republic of Ireland?

MARY MCALEESE

The first thing you have to do is stand for election; that usually
helps. So I stood for election in 1997. But you are right to
raise the question, because I was living in Northern Ireland
when I stood for election in the Republic of Ireland, and I was
working in Northern Ireland; and I did not have a vote in the

election in which I was elected. But thanks to the wording of the 1937 Irish Constitution, I as an Irish person and an Irish citizen am entitled to stand for election. So I stood. And the fact that I was from Northern Ireland didn't seem to have been held against me, thankfully. So I topped the poll and was elected. We serve for seven years: it's a seven-year term. Under the constitution, the president is entitled to serve a maximum of two terms. In 2004, I stood again for election, but unlike the first time in 1997 when there were five candidates, of whom one was a gentleman, the next time around I was unopposed. So that was a very easy election!

JOHN HALL

We are thinking about the Easter Rising a century ago. I'd like to ask you how you now see the events of the Easter Rising and how we should interpret them. It was a comparatively small event at the time but one of significance.

MARY MCALEESE

What happened of course on 24 April 1916, almost exactly half way through the Great War, was that a group of Irish men and women decided, effectively, to take on the might of the British Empire, using the words of the Proclamation that they read on that day from the General Post Office in what is now O'Connell Street in Dublin. They made a bid for freedom for the Irish people; they asserted in that Proclamation the right of the Irish people to decide their own destiny and the right to their own sovereignty. It was in that context that the Rising happened. It lasted about a week and, yes, it was very small, certainly in the scale of what was going on in the Great War. Over the course of that week just over 400 people died. Four hundred people could and did die often in two minutes in the Somme. So I suppose in the scale of things it was modest. At that time, it was not very well supported by the people, particularly in Dublin. But then a series of events happened which changed that.

The background to it was that there had been a very strong move in Parliament, by the Irish Party in Westminster, to push for home rule, and this had been a very fraught process. We should bear in mind that Ireland at that time was one unit administered as part of the United Kingdom. At the time, it looked as though Unionist resistance to home rule in the North of Ireland was going to result in the divided Ireland that, indeed, we now have. As a result, in 1914, Ireland had come to the brink of civil war because of the mobilization of the paramilitary Protestant Ulster volunteers in the North, which had in turn provoked the creation of the Nationalist Irish volunteers in the South. If it were not for the outbreak of World War One, historians tell us, Ireland would have descended into civil war in 1914. By 1916, those who believed in Ireland's right to independence from Britain did not believe that so-called 'home rule' through a devolved parliament in Dublin, and another in Belfast, would accord that right. They saw their opportunity: the Great War had not ended quickly as had been expected and it had become deeply unpopular. They chose their moment; they had their Rising. The Proclamation called on the Irish people to rally to the flag of Ireland to fight for sovereignty. Its language was modern even by today's standards. It talks of civil liberties, religious liberties, equal rights, equal opportunities, cherishing the children of the nation equally, referring to those in the North and those from the Anglican and British traditions all as children of the nation. And today in the

Republic of Ireland, for the first time since its foundation, we have Proclamation Day, when schools are invited to think on the Proclamation, interrogate it and imagine how they would translate that for a new generation and for a new future.

I am surely not going to look at the events of 1916 with the same eyes as someone who comes from the Unionist tradition, or the Protestant or Anglican traditions. We look at the same thing but we do not see it the same way. I look at empire. I've no pride in empire, any empire, Holy Roman Empire included. I think empires in general are not admirable; they are not based on admirable qualities. Ireland received the thick brunt of the British Empire. 1916 was the era of empires ending: the Russian Empire was going; the German Empire was about to go; the British Empire was fading. Irish men and women took on the might of the British Empire and challenged its right to own Ireland.

JOHN HALL

Do you think that there will come a time in this country when we regard 1916 in the same way that we regard 4 July 1776 in the United States?

MARY MCALEESE

I would like to think so. It is a legitimate comparison. Part of the problem historically is that the British and in particular the Unionists have regarded the Rising as treacherous, and this has coloured relationships between Ireland and Britain since that time. It was presumed that Irish men and women, by virtue of being part of the Empire, owed allegiance to the Empire. That thinking meant that we could sit down and have conversations together but we would miss each other by a mile. I grew up as an Irish Nationalist in Belfast and I remember one of the first conversations I ever had with Her Majesty the Queen, long before I became President. I explained to her that when she referred to her loyal subjects in Northern Ireland I always knew that I wasn't embraced by that phraseology, and I didn't particularly want to be. But neither did I want to be regarded as in any way a person who would justify the use of violence, in any regard, because of course I grew up through the Troubles. That puts you in a difficult place as well.

Back in 1916, there was not a huge amount of support for the Rising. The men of the Rising got a pretty hard time from the people of Dublin. But then the British response helped to set a trajectory of events that eventually led to the success of the Rising. First of all, seven people who signed the Proclamation, who are now regarded as the founding fathers of the Irish Republic, were summarily executed by the British at the beginning of May 1916. It is an interesting footnote that one of them, James Connelly, was born in Edinburgh and served in the British Army; another one, Thomas Clarke, was born on the Isle of Wight to a serving British soldier. So there were all sorts of strange connections. Their executions were regarded as cruel, mean and perverse, and they brought about an eruption of anger that eventually led, first of all, to the success of Sinn Féin. Whatever people say now, Sinn Féin took no part in the Rising, had nothing to do with it. But by 1918 Sinn Féin was essentially an embryonic political movement, which believed in the independence of Ireland and would not settle for anything less than independence. Sinn Féin overwhelmed the constitutional Irish Parliamentary Party in Westminster, wiping it off the face of the political map in 1918. Talk of introducing conscription in Ireland in 1918 had not helped the mood either: a political decision that threw oil on the fire, probably.

JOHN HALL

Thinking of movements to free a people, we have Nelson Mandela who decided, though not easily, that violence was justified, whereas Mahatma Gandhi refused to take that step. Where would you stand on that?

MARY MCALEESE

I think everybody at that time thought that violence was justified for just about everything. Violence was the default position of the world in so many respects. From this distance and as someone opposed to violence, I have no difficulty in saying that those men who fought in the Rising are my heroes. They founded the state I live in and of which I am very proud. But a lot of people take their legitimacy today from these men: democratic parties like Fine Gael and Fianna Fáil; constitutional politicians of all hues; *and* people who still continue to believe in the use of violence. Thankfully, nowadays they are much smaller in number, and really only fragments now. When I look at the Protestant-Unionist tradition in Ireland, the same elements exist in it. Carson and Craig, who are regarded as the fathers of Northern Unionism, were men who formed the paramilitary Ulster volunteers. They were involved in illegal gun running; they threatened the British establishment with violence unless they got their way. Today you have different spurs that came from that founding tradition: the spur that went into democratic peaceful politics; and the spur that maintained

Protestant Loyalist paramilitarism: just like those on the Catholic Republican side.

I think of someone like my own grandfather, who was an *aide de camp* to Eamon de Valera during the War of Independence and who was in the IRA. He took the opposite side to his brother, his only sibling, so there was a family tension for a long time around those politics. But I look at him and he was very typical, God rest him, now long since dead. As soon as the War was over, like most soldiers who return to civilian life, he became the most peaceful, law-abiding, democratic man. For him the call to arms was about getting through the eye of a very, very, very small needle, taking on the might of the Empire, creating an independent state. But what kind of state did he want? One that was peaceful and democratic.

JOHN HALL

This brings us now to consider the Peace Process. You've been tremendously committed to the Peace Process and to building bridges. Could I ask you, though, whether the process has led to significant change in Europe, in Ireland or simply superficial change?

MARY MCALEESE

Certainly not superficial; absolutely not superficial. I think it has led to the most profound change. I just look, for example, at the realm of compromise that had to be made on all sides in order to gather all those bits and pieces into the Good Friday Agreement. I think of politicians on all sides who really had to give the most courageous leadership and were not always thanked for doing so, who put their lives on the line, because the times were conflict- and violence-ridden. No, the change is very definitely not superficial. I think that would be to do it a great disservice. Anybody who lived through the Troubles will know that. There was then the historic overhang from partition, the exclusion, particularly in Northern Ireland, of Catholics from the political sphere, jobs, votes and housing, which prompted the civil rights demonstrations in the 1960s and the creation of, essentially, two confessional states. I believe confessional states are very unhealthy places and they were, indeed, very unhealthy places. People were fearful of one another: they had conflicting religions and very different political ambitions. They had to inhabit the same space with its undertow of violence. Given all of that, I think the people of Northern Ireland, and the politicians of Northern Ireland, achieved a remarkable thing in the Good Friday Agreement.

JOHN HALL

It is astonishing to think of Ian Paisley shaking hands with Gerry Adams and Martin McGuinness. What gave rise to it, what sparked the process?

MARY MCALEESE

A desire for peace. First of all, not everybody was involved in violence; not everybody supported violence. The vast majority of people in Northern Ireland, whether they are Catholic or Protestant, come out of a Christian tradition, which is a prayerful tradition, a tradition that desires peace. So there were many good people who never lifted a gun in their lives or ever supported a bomb or a bullet and who tried their best to live decent lives. They sometimes get forgotten in the equation. They were the ballast, they were the cantilever and they were the people who ultimately, I think, put pressure on the politicians and the political leaders to do their very best to try to bring about a resolution that would give us a peaceful future.

In the 1980s, a Redemptorist priest called Father Alex Reid, a Tipperary man, was based in a Belfast monastery called Clonard on the Falls Road, the Republican heartland of Belfast but also right beside the Loyalist heartland on the Shankhill Road. He visited the prisons a lot and talked to the prisoners. He began to intuit among the Republican prisoners a great tiredness: many of them were in prison for a generation. He intuited their tiredness and a kind of a feeling that they couldn't win and they couldn't lose. The British had arrived at the same feeling: that they couldn't win and couldn't lose. Fr Reid asked himself: where were we going to go with this? He is the person who brought John Hume and Gerry Adams together in the hope that John Hume could persuade Adams that a democratic and constitutional alternative was possible. Hume is *the* outstanding champion of peace, democratic politics, constitutional politics, very much in the tradition of that great liberator and champion of human rights and democracy of the early nineteenth century, Daniel O'Connell. The idea of a peace process carved out through the ballot box started there.

JOHN HALL

Am I right to suggest that the process really got going because it was possible to have behind-the-scenes conversations of that kind that you couldn't possibly have with the media watching?

MARY MCALEESE

We wouldn't have a Peace Process without those conversations. People, especially politicians, say all sorts of things,
such as, for example, that they won't talk to terrorists. The
one person who used to say that most often, Margaret
Thatcher, also made sure there were back channels to those
very terrorists. Of course, there have to be back channels.
Louise Richardson, currently Vice-Chancellor of the
University of Oxford, is an expert in this area and in the area
of dealing with the world of terrorists. She just says very
simply, from all her research, that if you want peace, you
have to talk to your enemy, because it is with your enemy
that you have to make peace. That is not to say that those
talks are upfront and personal but you do create conduits and
in and out of those conduits comes a realization of what is
possible. Very often, in the public space, people will put
their position at its most extreme. When you are working to
promote compromise, you have to find what, in back of that
hard public line, are they willing to sacrifice.

JOHN HALL

When the most extreme politicians on both sides are elected,
they cannot be outflanked, and that makes the Peace Process
possible. Is that a right reading?

MARY MCALEESE

Well, it's a jump ahead. Let's remember that the Democratic
Unionist Party, who now lead the Government of Northern
Ireland under the Good Friday Agreement, was not in favour
of the Good Friday Agreement and originally took no part
in its design. David Trimble was one of the architects of

the Good Friday Agreement. He really put his life on the line and sacrificed a lot for the Peace because extremists who counted him as theirs saw him compromising. So in a sense the extremists, if you want to call them that, came from very well-populated and well-supported margins. They put a lot of stress and pressure on the more central politicians, who between them, and despite the extremes, were able to gather the critical mass sufficient to generate the momentum that led to the Good Friday Agreement. And in doing that they gave leadership to those who were more fearful, more oppositional, more dyed in the wool, more die hard. The work of the central politicians softened the hearts behind them, and at the same time hardened the political ground, so that people could walk on it safely. It was the work of very courageous politicians, and indeed of some of the paramilitaries who were converted from being driven by the use of violence to using the democratic process. That didn't always endear them to their constituencies either, regrettably: many of them had to pay a price for that. I do think that imaginative political leadership was important as was the *real politik* of the moment. This was the realization that you were entitled to go and ask those people who were constantly saying that they wanted peace and that they desired peace, 'what price are you prepared to pay for it?' You don't get a resolution like the Good Friday Agreement unless people are prepared to compromise. I come from a very pragmatic way of looking at these things: 90 per cent of something is better than 100 per cent of nothing. And violence is 100 per cent of nothing. The Good Friday Agreement was a 90 per cent deal and a pathway to peace. A good deal.

JOHN HALL

If we think about the role of culture and religion, we start to think more deeply about repairing divisions. How profound is the repair? Have hearts and minds been changed? Is Ireland really different now as a result of the Peace Process?

MARY MCALEESE

I think that these islands and not just Ireland are different now as a result of the Peace Process. We have done something useful, for we have shown that if you want to make peace, the first thing you have to do is really to interrogate your own position. And in a conflict situation we are not very good at that; we get very complacent about our own position, but boy do we have a PhD done on the position of the other. And so exercised are we about the position of the other that we don't devote very much time to examining our own position. And I think one of the reasons why the change was profound was that we all began to interrogate our own positions, our view of history. We began to stand more and more in the feet of the other and look at the world with the eyes of the other with the realization that we were missing each other by a mile. Unionists and Nationalists in Northern Ireland could live cheek by jowl thinking they knew a lot about each other, enough to be mutually contemptuous about each other, but actually the truth is that we lived in very great ignorance of each other's narrative. We were looking at the world with lenses that do not see the world the same way.

I expressed that view in a very simple remark when Her Majesty the Queen came to Ireland in May 2011. In my own words, I referred to the colonizer and the colonized and how they look differently at the world. On that state visit, the one thing we did not do was miss each other by a mile. In her remarkable, historic speech at the state dinner, the Queen said the words 'A Uachtaráin agus a chairde', which translates just very simply as 'President and friends'. Anybody who knows the history of Ireland, and the history of the Irish language, will know the huge efforts that had been made, particularly in the nineteenth century in imperial Ireland, to destroy the Irish language, and in so doing to dismantle the power of Irish culture. I knew, the moment she used those words, that hearts that were quite hard against British Empire, monarchy and Britain would melt. Even those words themselves were deeply egalitarian. There was no rehearsal of the usual formula 'distinguished lords and ladies, ladies and gentlemen'. She just said 'President and friends'. I knew those words would melt hearts, because here was someone who was not simply a very high level tourist coming to see us, but someone on a mission of reconciliation.

JOHN HALL

If religion was the cause of division, how could it then be the cause of change? Was it, at all, the cause of change?

MARY MCALEESE

Yes, I think it has been. It's part of the mix. People argue this all the time: were the divisions political, constitutional, religious? Division was a cord of many strands and religion is in there. One of the most sensible things said about it many years ago was by Conor Cruise O'Brien when he was asked whether religion in Northern Ireland was a red herring, and he said that if it was, it was the size of a whale. So, that'll give you some idea. Yes, we can't escape from the toxicity of Reformation and Counter Reformation politics. Religious politics are still being played out on the streets of Northern Ireland, indeed on these islands: it's an issue. I think we had to work our way through all of that. Were we courageous enough, given that we are talking out of two Christian traditions? No, we weren't. Some people were; there were some wonderful exemplars of Christian outreach from both communities. But as a general rule, because I think we go to separate schools, separate workplaces, separate communities, 90 per cent of people who live in Northern Ireland live in areas that are defined by religion. On the religious front, in terms of making that whale smaller, we probably didn't do enough and we could have done a lot more.

On the other hand, there were a lot of things happening in parallel. In the 1960s, the Catholic Church internationally had opened up; we were coming out of what was essentially another empire. In 1870, the Pope was still both Emperor of the Papal States and spiritual leader; the temporal papal empire was about to end but it took decades for that reality to sink in. Then Pope John XXIII brought about the Second Vatican Council, calling for *novus habitus mentis*, a new mental culture, a new way of looking at the world. It was a great ecumenical event with many people from other religious traditions invited to be present. And then I remember when Pope Paul gave Archbishop Michael Ramsey his episcopal ring. I'm a frequent visitor to the Anglican Centre in Rome, and I remember going up the stairs one day and into the room and seeing that picture there, and it just brought me back to that time of great hope. Somewhere along the way we lost that hope. And in 1950, when John XXIII was Papal Nuncio to France, a big conference took place in Luxeuil in France, on the 1400th anniversary of the sixth-century genius St Columbanus, who is a huge part of the intellectual patrimony of Europe. At that conference, there was a private meeting in a hotel at which were present the major architects of what eventually became the European Union, first the European Community. There were no minutes of that meeting; there is no record of it; it was a private meeting. There members of the British Government, members of the Irish Government, members of governments who had been neutral during the War, all of the participants who had been on the Allied and Axis sides, they were all represented, all gathered, so that Schumann's and Monet's great idea could be aired: the idea of *totius Europae*. All of Europe working together in partnership, to preserve the peace but a peace that would become much more than an absence of war. A peace through partnership that would give the children of Europe, the young people of Europe, something really visionary and new. The idea became the European Union but it was first conceived 1400 years ago by the great Irish St Columbanus, of Bangor monastery fame, when he coined the phrase *totius Europae* and said it was possible to be Irish, French, German, English and also European and that this was possible if people stopped fighting with each other so as to work together and feel the surging power that comes from partnership.

The example of what the European Union accomplished out of the disaster of two world wars was playing and working through the minds of a lot of people from Northern Ireland, particularly people from both sides of the so-called religious divide. A lot of people tried their best to bridge the gaps. I think of Corrymeela, I think of the Protestant ecumenist Reverend Cecil Kerr, one of my great mentors, a man whom I just absolutely adored, I think of the work that was done in Clonard Monastery to try and create spaces for people who belong to Christian denominations but who had in their hearts fear of another Christian denomination, even possibly hatred. And there were a lot of people who worked on that quietly, relentlessly, hopefully.

JOHN HALL

To build change, to create change...

MARY MCALEESE

...and that change is genuine. To be honest I do think that the toxic spores of sectarianism, any ism – racism, sectarianism, sexism, homophobia, whatever – they've a very long shelf life and there are always people who make it their business to take the spores and make sure they are cast ahead into the next generation. And what we have learnt now, I think, again this answers your question about the profundity of change, we have learnt that you really do have to take out those weeds, dig out those toxic deeds and stop their transmission into the future. You can't let the chaff grow up with the wheat, you cannot let those seeds germinate; you do actually have to root them out.

JOHN HALL

In your own role, your personal commitment to this achievement, did you ever feel that sometimes this was too much to achieve, that it was impossible? And if you did feel that at any point, what did you turn to for help to achieve your goal of building bridges?

MARY MCALEESE

There were always actually practical things. I remember the worst day for me, in all the 14 years in office, was the day of the Omagh bomb. There's just nothing compares with it, except maybe one other day, which was the day I was married. At our last wedding anniversary, Martin went off to play golf. We don't celebrate our wedding anniversary, because on the morning of our wedding, two of my dearest friends were murdered. They were two Catholic brothers. They were killed by Loyalists in their little restaurant. They had petrol poured over them and then they were set fire to, and they died. So, we don't celebrate because that was a pretty horrific day. The very next day the IRA carried out a retaliatory killing, which is what you got: tit for tat, a zero-sum game except of course for 1000 per cent misery in every family affected. By God's good grace I met the daughter of the man who died in retaliation for my friends' deaths some years later. We bonded immediately, thanks to the same overwhelming grief, and the same view of the absolutely craven stupidity and wastefulness of all those deaths. So I kept a photo on my desk of my beautiful, gentle, murdered friends, Tony and Miles O'Reilly. I kept their pictures on my desk for 14 years that I was in office, as a daily reminder that anything I could do to prevent days like that ever from happening, I would have to do.

So what we did was really very simple and human. We had a lot of cups of tea, a lot of dinners, lots of lunches, because the president's role is really a pastoral role, it's in that space, that moral, pastoral space. And there was no point in us sitting for 14 years talking to people who agreed with us. We had to show in every way possible, in the words of the Proclamation, that we could and did cherish the children of the nation equally, even those who did not want to be part of the nation. We wanted to cherish people, but not in a proselytizing way. One of the dangers that came from both of our Christian traditions, particularly in Northern Ireland, but it's true generally I think, is that we came out of evangelical, proselytizing traditions, both politically and spiritually. We thought the other was so misguided that if we could only talk to them for ten minutes they would convert to our position. And that was a dangerous phenomenon, because there's no respect in that really for the otherness of the other and the right of the other to be as other as they want to be. So what we decided to do was to make our house a place where we could begin to be good neighbours with people who did not want to come anywhere near our house because we were the other and we were the enemy. So we had to work very hard to try to peel away those layers of distrust and we did that over a period.

And then there was Omagh: as evil as it is possible to get. I went up the next day to Omagh, though the security advice was adamant I shouldn't go. I was equally adamant that there was nowhere else I could be. So I went, and I remember the then chairman of the local council, a mighty man, a really good guy, a member of the Unionist fraternity, and I just remember hugging him and the two of us hugging each other. I was so glad that he hugged me, and he told me he was glad I hugged him, and I remember being at the funeral, David Trimble was there as well, and the great sense of human solidarity and shared grief. I just felt, look I'm your bog-standard Irish Nationalist and there are probably things in my head, in my baggage and in my thinking that will drive a Unionist neighbour mad, and *vice versa*, and is it possible that we can still be friends? Could we still be friends, could we still be good neighbours, could we still be colleagues? Could we still offer each other warmth and affection and the promise of never using violence against each other and the promise of never trying to turn each other into me or one into the other? And I think we can do that, and we have set down the road of doing that, so that is what we did, my husband and I, for the 14 years in office.

After the Good Friday Agreement was signed and the violence began to dwindle, there were still very dangerous fragments of groups wedded to violence. One of these fragments carried out the killing of two young soldiers in Massereene Barracks. Martin, my husband, had given up his job to work full time on building up this new culture of good neighbourliness and in particular working with the Loyalist paramilitaries, a difficult but important constituency. Martin knew from dealing with them that their initial response to the killing would be anger, and the danger was that they would get into tit for tat killings and that if we got into that then we would end up behind the sectarian barricades again. Martin did an extraordinary thing. He sat on the phone for 24 hours and he called every single Loyalist paramilitary that he knew, begging them not to retaliate. There was no retaliation. Subsequently, the Secretary of State publicly remarked on the importance of Martin's intervention. Martin's connection with that constituency of estranged Loyalists began with cups of tea. I also think it's important that when you're having the tea and buns, you don't get down to immediate political agendas because, frankly, certainly in the early days of the Troubles, neither politicians nor people were equipped with the language of nuance, and we were not equipped with a kind of warm neighbourly tone. We were more likely to use, if we'd got into politics, the language of contempt and the language of confrontation: this is what we were more practised in. Nowadays we are much more practised in the language of warmth and tone, and we are much more aware that language can have consequences: it can open hearts or it can close hearts and we've learnt all those lessons the bitter and the hard way.

JOHN HALL

Mary, thank you very much, you've given us an enormous amount. And you're an example for us, not only in what you've achieved, but also the courage and determination and commitment that does achieve those great things. So thank you very much indeed.

AUDIENCE QUESTIONER

I grew up in Armagh, in the middle of the Troubles and spent the first three years of my working life bringing Protestant and Catholic children together in Lurgan. I simply want to say 'thank you'. As a Methodist youth worker, you invited my youth group, and we had those tea and buns. I remember some pretty good scones as well. As a Protestant in Northern Ireland, I want to say thank you for the way you used your office to build bridges on our island. And the question I want to ask you is – the kids I worked with loved the same football teams, loved the same music, but they went to different schools. They went to different schools, they lived in different parts of town, they never met each other. Is integrated education the way forward for the people of Northern Ireland?

MARY MCALEESE

This is one that comes up really regularly. I think that when people live in a divided community, it's important to look at what the sources of the division are, what they are divided about. I think that's why the politics are so important, because the politics handle what people are divided about. And when people are divided so passionately about these things, I think what you get inevitably is what we have: divided communities, divided spaces, no shared spaces, no community spaces that are shared, including schools. If I look back through the Troubles, do I think that integrated education would have helped? I'm not sure that the children would have been capable of handling the profundity of what was going on around them and it might have been a big deal. But I think the integrated sector, and the reason there is a passion for the integrated sector is a good sign, a sign that people want a shared space, want to get to know one another, want to break out. On the other hand, I have to say that I believe in the human right of people to make their own choices about education and the right to have your denominational or whatever other kind of education you want for your child. In the Republic of Ireland there is a very big debate going on about this at the moment, in a slightly different way from whether integrated education could contribute to the building of a new society in Northern Ireland. Yes, I believe that a developing integrated sector is going to parallel what it is hoped is happening in the political space, and also, more importantly, will help to drive what's happening in the political space. But as I look at what's happening in the Republic, where 90 per cent of primary schools are currently Catholic schools, now that about 15–16 per cent of the people who inhabit the Republic of Ireland are not born on the island of Ireland, there is an increasing demand for a greater educational diversity: faith-based, non-faith, secular, inter-faith, ecumenical, all sorts of different patterns. The Catholic Archbishop of Dublin has supported the Government's move towards greater educational diversity.

Martin and I are both products of denominational education in Northern Ireland. I was educated by Mercy and Dominican nuns, and Martin by the Christian brothers. They gave us a great education. In no way would I describe it as sectarian, but I would certainly describe it as denominational.

JOHN HALL

You can build links between different schools and then people experience other ways of life.

MARY MCALEESE

And you can share campuses. I worry, going back to the question, whether we should have had integrated education during the Troubles. I don't believe in using education for the purpose of achieving through children what adults can't achieve through political endeavour.

AUDIENCE QUESTIONER

I'm an ethnic Albanian, living in London. Whenever I think of the conflict between Northern Ireland and Ireland, I think of the Kosovo and Serbian conflict. When it comes to Albanians and Serbians, I would say that mainly what keeps them so hateful towards each other is patriotism, as well as religion, but I believe patriotism is far more to be blamed when it comes to creating conflict with each other than religion. And the reason I say that is because in 2004 Albanians burned down nearly every single Serbian [Orthodox] church in Kosovo, but they did not touch one Catholic [non-Serbian] church at all.

MARY MCALEESE

Interesting that you should mention Kosovo, because what came into my mind when we were talking about integrated education was a programme that followed from the break-up of the Yugoslav Republic, a programme on television talking to Muslim women who had been raped. They were so free with the names of those who raped them. The journalist said to them, 'You seem to know the people who raped you. How do you know those people?' And the answer was quite chilling, 'Because we went to school with them.' That frightened me. Because of course Tito's claim was that he had integrated Christian and Muslim within an education system. So it is very important what people are taught, as well as where and with whom they are taught. And you're right about patriotism to this extent; I don't think patriotism is all that bad a thing, I think jingoism is a terrible thing, but I think to have a pride in your country is a good thing, and to create a country to be proud of is a good thing. But nasty jingoism, no. Something that moves us towards hubris and moves us towards a hatred of others is an ugly thing. But pride in a decent country, a good country, a caring country, a welcoming country is not a bad thing. I would agree with you that in Ireland and Northern Ireland, through our troubles, there were different forms of patriotism at work. One was an Irish Nationalism; one was a form of British Nationalism: a love of all things British. The other was a love of all things Irish, you could say. One of the things we've learnt in more recent times in Northern Ireland and Ireland generally, I think north and south, is not to be so precious about those labels. I grew up as an Irish person in British Belfast but in an environment that had the familiarity of home. Living in London, Martin and I find everything is familiar, everything is comfortable because it's like living where I grew up. Our nations rub off each other and we leave some imprint and I think it's important to acknowledge the good imprint we can leave on one another. One of the lovely imprints on my life was the opportunity to live in Rome, in a centre with 20 students, a multi-faith centre, with a young Imam from Kosovo, who is now a good friend and my global adviser on all things Muslim, and that was a fantastic opportunity to live as I did with a young Imam and another Imam from Côte d'Ivoire, with a Jewish Rabbi, a Dervish nun, members of the Orthodox Church, members of Eastern Rite Catholics – that great mix. Maybe we should force integrated *adult* education.

JOHN HALL

Are there lessons that could be learnt from the Irish changes that ought to be applied to the Middle East at the moment?

MARY MCALEESE

I am always very hesitant to think that we have achieved something that is so nailed shut and has got such clear edges that you can just pick it up and hand it to someone else and say here's the template. Not for nothing is what we have done called a process, a peace process. But I do think there are human elements to it that are transferrable. I talked a moment ago about tone, and I will be interested to see the academic work that eventually comes out of the Northern Ireland Peace Process, because there has been a change in the quality of discourse, political discourse, and that has been really important. I would credit someone like George Mitchell with a lot of that, a very serene and temperate man – how he stayed serene and how he stayed temperate I don't know, but he did when he was President Clinton's special adviser on Northern Ireland. He used a language of political engagement, he introduced a graciousness into the language of politics. I do think that political discourse benefits from graciousness, from mutual graciousness, not just graciousness to one's own but graciousness particularly to the other, for this reason: in a conflict situation we are educated from a very young age to be sensitive to slights that come from the other, and when we hear barbed language, our hearts harden. When you have hardened hearts, it's very hard to build consensus, and it's very hard to come out of conflict. I find the same in those parts of the world particularly where there is toxic conflict around identity, whether it's religious identity, whether it's the identity of nation or ethnicity. That barbed language is dangerous, it is toxic, it's what carries the spores into the next generation. And it makes hardened hearts grow in the little babies who are born in today's hospitals, and they become the angry men and women of tomorrow. I think that to talk to one another is important, to critique one's own position is important and to be hard on oneself and one's history and one's narrative is important, seeking to extract from it a fuller truth, because everybody ransacks history for ammunition that shows the perversity of the other and reflects well on our own side.

AUDIENCE QUESTIONER

Like yourself I'm an Ulster woman. What would you say about Brexit in relation to the Irish Peace Process?

MARY MCALEESE

It's no secret, I'm very strongly pro European Union, and it's a strange thing in a way. Why am I so strongly in favour of it? I just regard it as the most important bulwark for peace. I was born in the immediate aftermath of the Second World War, so in my parents' generation there were a lot of old soldiers around my area, for while the Republic had been neutral, Northern Ireland, where I am from, had been part of the war effort. We had American soldiers based not far from where my parents lived. I grew up with all those post World War films, but the most important thing for me is the number who died, tens and tens and tens of millions. And I've been to the war graves, and I'm the mother of a 30-year-old son, and I think of all the mothers of those times whose sons never got to 30 years of age, who got to 18, 19, 20, who have little crosses marking their graves, because they were sent off to war in their tens of millions because Europe's default position was war. We're talking France, we're talking Germany, we're talking Russia, we're talking the United Kingdom, we're talking places that we go for weekends on holidays now. A new generation knows none of this from first principles. The European Union is the bulwark against war and, more importantly, overlaying that, it is the opportunity to know the power of partnership and how difficult partnership is. War is easier than peace. One of the things that we've learnt is that making peace is not easy, maintaining peace is not easy and so the European Union is the idea, the concept, the inspiration of fundamentally keeping peace on this European continent that broke itself apart and wasted life so shamefully in the first half of the twentieth century. The EU is an insurance policy to make sure that doesn't happen again and that's why it's so important. Britain's contribution to that has been extraordinary, absolutely extraordinary. It has been one of the pillars of the Union. It came into the Union the same day as Ireland did in 1973. Did it speak with the same voice as the other 27 countries? No, but the beauty about that Brussels table is that it is a table around which people try to work out problems and have templates and have treaties and have structure, rather like the Good Friday Agreement. The European Union is about not leaving peace to chance.

You asked me about the Peace Process in this regard. There is no doubt in my mind that membership of the European Union made a seminal difference, a critical difference to the relationship between Irish and British politicians, and it helped to create a much greater mood of collegiality out of which came the shared effort, the shared stewardship, you could say, of the Peace Process and the protagonists of the Peace Process. So in many ways the Peace Process in Northern Ireland is a child of the European Union. I think the European Union can assert a sort of maternity and paternity in the Peace Process, it's a kind of exemplar.

AUDIENCE QUESTIONER

There are some in Scotland who want to stay in Europe but leave the United Kingdom. And this raises for me some interesting issues about community. It seems to me that perhaps community is a matter of not only boundary, but also identity and interest.

MARY MCALEESE

I won't make a comment about Scotland, but I will say this: that identity is very powerful. It was missed, if we go back to where we started this conversation, in 1916. Many people who were looking at what happened in 1916 missed the issue of Irish identity. They presumed that since loyalty to Empire was what was demanded, it would happen. I'm reminded very much of when Madeleine Albright was writing her memoirs, one of the things that she commented on was about the Iranian religious revolution in the mid 1970s. A sensible person in the Central Intelligence Agency (CIA) had said to his boss, 'Do you think we really should try and figure out the impact of religion in Iran and how important it is to Iran?' And the CIA boss said, don't be ridiculous, religion is dead, or words to that effect. Anyway, there was no interrogation of the religious sensibilities and sensitivities and identity in Iran, with the result that when the Iranian religious revolution happened, the Americans were completely wrong footed, completely taken by surprise, because nobody had probed what was beneath the surface, what was happening in the subterranean world of the spirit, the gut, the emotion, the heart. And so in Ireland it had been going on for centuries, the development of a contra-identity, an identity that was contrary to the ambient identity of the British Empire. That was in the ether, it was a *leitmotif*, but the structures of society didn't really allow it to penetrate all the way through. So people lived with a sense of both complacency and, I suppose, denial, or at least a failure to recognize.

It came home to me in a conversation a few years ago in a restaurant in Spain. We were with Spanish friends, and the issue of the Basque country came up, and oh boy there was an explosive discussion. One man kept banging the table and saying that they are 600 years a part of Spain, how can they talk about a separate identity? And when he eventually calmed down I told him, I'm Irish, I can understand how they can talk about a separate identity. We were part of the British Empire, and indeed part of this United Kingdom for many centuries, but there was another river of identity running also, very powerfully, and eventually it ran to full flood. This is why I say we need to interrogate the otherness of others so that we don't miss these rivers that run deep in people. I think you are very right, identity is powerful, it's a very powerful marker for people. I'd like to think, though, that we could use identity not to build walls to keep others out, but in our confidence in identity, part of the pride we would have in our identity is that our primary identity is as human beings who can care for the other. No matter who he is, no matter who she is, we can care for them and welcome them. And certainly, those of us who identify ourselves and who overlay our national identities with our Christian beliefs, I'd like to think the latter is our primary identity, that the question of who we are finds a response in the Christian message. For me it just boils down to Christ's Great Commandment to love one another. And it's the merging of those parallel identities and not letting the political identity become some form of poison.

JOHN HALL

That is marvellous point at which to conclude this remarkable dialogue. What we have discovered, ladies and gentlemen, is that behind this brilliant mind is a very committed soul. Within the extraordinary achievement of being President, re-elected unopposed for a second term, is a person who learns from experience, who has a degree of humility and the power to listen, and a wonderful nuance and wonderful tone in the way she addresses issues. We are truly grateful, Mary, for your presence with us, and truly grateful for what you achieved during your years as President and in so many other ways. And we wish to express our very warm thanks to you but also wish you every blessing in your continuing ministry as Ireland continues to change and the process goes on to bring people together in a very full way. And we can learn the lessons internationally from this seminal experience where the seeds are no longer toxic spores but the seeds of growth: healthy spores. Thank you.

Idealism and Compromise

Three Essays by Vernon White

Introduction

The three essays that follow belong best as a connected sequence. They each explore a positive feature of human experience (our idealism, our sense of morality, our persistent purposefulness) and then reflect on their deeper implications. What does it mean to take these seriously in a world that frequently frustrates them? How and why do they retain meaning and authority for us when the realities of the world and public life often seem to thwart them? These are human questions for us all. But they are often particularly acute for those who work in public roles and in public service.

The essays also reflect specifically on the ultimate origin and grounds of these human experiences. In that sense, they attempt to exemplify one of the core aims of the Westminster Abbey Institute, as described in the Introduction. They assume that many in public life as a matter of fact do have genuine moral commitments. But the purpose is not then to go 'forwards' from these moral commitments into specific policy-making – which is ground well covered by others.

The aim here instead is to go 'backwards' from these commitments into their ultimate ground: to uncover their deepest drivers. These drivers, it seems to me, lie in metaphysics and wider religious world-views, not just in sociology or biology.

To recognize this is important in its own right. But it is also important because it can become a gateway to find new resources for sustaining our moral commitments. By owning a wider world-view that makes sense of moral commitments we will find new motivation and support for them – especially in particular situations that compromise them. In other words, this invitation to go 'backwards' into the origins of our best ideals and purposes is not really backwards after all: it is a way of going forwards – better equipped.

IDEALISM

*Exploring the Implications
of Our Thwarted Ideals*

I want to confront a conundrum as old as the hills: a dilemma experienced sharply in public life, but not exclusively, because it is also part of everyone's life. It is the experience of having ideals that we cannot make happen. It is the experience of thwarted visionaries, when 'our eyes can see further than our hands can reach' as Karl Deutsch said of Karl Jaspers' philosophy (Jaspers 1952, p.18). It occurs when the irresistible force of idealism hits the immoveable rocks of reality and has to be compromised.

This experience, I suspect, *matters* to many of us; it niggles, haunts, even though we may think we have become hardened realists who can shrug our shoulders and say that is just the way life is. It matters because moral ideals are too deeply embedded in our human identity simply to ignore. Whether you attribute this moral idealism to the Spirit of God within us, or just to socio-biological factors, either way we still have these ideals and they matter to us. I believe this is true of more public figures than sceptics might think. Former US Secretary of State Henry Kissinger, for example, has been widely thought to epitomize just soulless pragmatism and realism. But his recent memoir *World Order* (Kissinger 2015) tells a different story. There, as Hillary Clinton has said, 'the famous realist sounds surprisingly idealistic'. Niall Fergusson (2015) has made the same point. Kissinger was constantly bringing moral principles to bear on his calculations about power. It consistently mattered to him to do so. It also mattered when he found it hard to do.

It is a dilemma, moreover, that never goes away. Ideals will always matter because they cannot be shrugged off without losing our soul; compromises will always be inevitable because, as I shall argue, it is the very nature and structure of reality that frustrates these ideals, not just our moral failings.

So my purpose in exploring it is certainly not to pretend we can ever avoid the dilemma. Nor, incidentally, is it an attempt to offer criteria to help us distinguish good and bad compromises, something well covered elsewhere (Margalit 2010). But it is an attempt to explore the underlying implications of the dilemma. I want to ask what this persistence of compromised ideals *means*. What does it mean about the ultimate nature of the world? What, therefore, does that mean about the sort of persons we must be to operate realistically in such a world, without just becoming cynical?

To try to answer these questions I will draw on analysis from philosophy, theology and literature. But first, three brief illustrations of thwarted idealism, deliberately diverse, to help show the range of issues involved.

First, an experience from the First World War trenches, a snapshot from the celebrated but fleeting Christmas truce of 1914. It was a brief moment when the opposing sides stopped firing, some played football with each other and they exchanged presents. It generated some striking expressions of idealism, most notably by one of the many soldiers who later turned to writing, Henry Williamson (Williamson 1969). He wrote of his belief that this brief cessation of slaughter that he had experienced was actually a sign of universal hope. It signalled the inevitable triumph of peace over conflict; the conviction that all disputes would ultimately be resolved.

What is notable is the sheer scale of this sort of idealism. It expresses a belief that all people are fundamentally peaceful and rational and could always come to agree. If we read Williamson's back story, this becomes even clearer. He believed that even Hitler might have absorbed that spirit of the football match when he was in the trenches. This meant that later in the 1930s Williamson did not think there could ever be another war. Incredibly, he held to this idea not only through the Somme and Passchendaele, and through the Second World War, but also right through the Vietnam war. All these bloody battles palpably discredited his belief, yet he held to it. It is an extraordinary testimony to the sheer power of idealism to persist.

But as such it is also an example of one of the key issues of the dilemma: namely, how some idealism can only persist by hardening into an immature fantasy, skewing reality to fit the ideals, in this case even to the extent of imagining Hitler to be a potential saviour. Few read Williamson today: you do not get much oxygen of publicity for an extreme view like that. But it is a cast of mind we do sometimes still meet, even if in less extreme forms. When, for example, it was said of UK politician Tony Benn's lifelong idealism that he 'immatured' as he got older (rather than maturing like other people), this may or may not be entirely fair: the context and politics were different and so was the man. But it indicates at least a perception of a similar mindset. And it raises this key issue: how can ideals be maintained *without* fantasy?

The second illustration is from peacetime. This is provided not by a soldier-poet of the maverick right in a war but liberal-left political philosopher Bernard Williams (2014). He too was an idealist, but his idealism operated quite differently. There is no specific experience lying behind his view, so far as I know, just a lifetime's disposition of idealism born of a political creed. In his case, this was socialism: he was convinced that socialism is a genuinely egalitarian form of politics, the only systematic political thought that could secure egalitarian civil rights, health care and education. He too persisted with this overall commitment even when these ideals were compromised by events (as they were). But, crucially, when thwarted he did not fantasize; he simply modified his ideals. He continued to support socialism, but accepted that its most optimistic forms must nevertheless adapt. He realized that the human values underlying it cannot always *all* be rendered compatible in particular situations and policies.

What lies behind the difference? Social, political and personal contexts clearly played their part. The academic Williams had tried to move from academia to public service to try out his ideals in practical policy but made his move into public life at almost the exact time that Margaret Thatcher's Government came to power, when the 1960s and 70s changed to the 80s: hardly a propitious time for any kind of socialist agenda.

But it was not just the difficult political context that made him adapt his ideals. It was the fact that Williams was now trying to act out his theories in real public policy. It was also, I suspect, simply because he had a different cast of mind. For when Williams came up against this political fact of a changed and obdurate government, he did not see it just as a contingent fact that happened to make his ideals impossible in practice at that time. He looked beneath these contingencies and seemed to see something about the nature of reality itself that makes human values incompatible *in principle*, not just in practice, a view shared by fellow political philosopher Isaiah Berlin. What happens when ideals seem impossible in principle, not just in particular circumstances, therefore becomes another issue to probe. It implicitly raises questions of metaphysics, not just of practical morals or indeed of psychology. Williams himself eventually retreated back into academia to pursue these questions.

A third illustration of idealism comes from a different context again. Here the experience underlying it is neither war nor a debate on systematic political ideology but just a minor domestic incident. It occurs in small-town Texas when a young man returned home from Yale to discover his father had been building him a rifle as an act of love for him ('meticulously carving the stock and boring the barrel... beautifully made, as only a craftsman could do', a biographer records (Cavanaugh 2001, p.20)). The trouble is that the young man has returned with new ideals. So the biographer also has to record his conflicted reaction. On the one hand he has to tell his father (somewhat brutally) that wise social policy means 'someday we are going to have to take these goddammed things away from you people' (Cavanaugh 2001, p.20). Yet crucially, on the other hand, even as he says this, he also realizes 'he still had not done the right thing' (Cavanaugh 2001, p.21).

It is a familiar enough scenario: a bright young person is caught in transition between a traditional, small-town conservative upbringing and new values gained elsewhere; he first shoots (metaphorically) from the hip, then realizes life is not so simple. *Prima facie* it is just another example of Williams' perception that one set of ideals sometimes conflicts with another in principle – in this case, ideals of pacifism conflicting with values of personal relationship like grace and gratitude. Yet there is also something else going on here; something that may or may not have been true for Williams but here is absolutely explicit. There is a clear sense that neither set of values can be jettisoned *without deep regret* ('he still had not done the right thing'). In other words, he needed to know how both sets of values could coexist not just as an intellectual exercise but also as part of a personal moral imperative. In fact, he felt this so acutely that it became a catalyst for a lifetime's effort as an ethicist to resolve this (an effort resulting in a theory and practice of living where this tension is held together in a person's character and an overall narrative, rather than in isolated actions).

But that is to anticipate. For now, I just want to use these examples to highlight the common thread that runs through them, the common questions they raise. For in these different reactions – the poet who kept his ideals but denied reality; the political philosopher who adapted his ideals but in the end withdrew from public life; and the ethicist trying to hold together conflicting ideals – we see thwarted idealism played out in different contexts yet all begging these same underlying questions. Namely, *why* do ideals always get compromised? Why do values sometimes conflict? What does this mean about the nature of reality itself? What, in turn, does that mean about ourselves and how we should respond to it? And since these are questions for which philosophy and theology, as much as psychology or practical ethics, seem most relevant, that is how I will now proceed. I will turn for help first to a philosopher and then to some theology.

Karl Jaspers and some philosophical insights

Karl Jaspers was a twentieth-century German philosopher with a wide-ranging professional and intellectual background. Vitally, he had also encountered the dilemma of compromise at first hand. In his experience of the Second World War he had lived in constant fear himself because of his Jewish connections and then worked in the aftermath of the War with survivors scarred with a sense of guilt and inadequacy. At first, he tried to use his background in law, medicine and psychiatry to get a purchase on the dilemma. But it was not enough. So that is when he turned to philosophy. He also turned to the literary genre of tragedy where the experience of compromised idealism is most searingly portrayed, but where he also found insight to see beyond the impasse and where he also came to see that 'tragedy is not enough' (Jaspers 1952).

But how did he reach this point? First, his analysis of the dilemma and then his venture beyond.

In his analysis he identified three reasons for the dilemma, all rooted in the fundamental structure of ourselves and the world. The first is that we are naturally actors in life, not just observers, and it is when we act to make things happen that our limits become most apparent. In terms of Williamson's wartime metaphor, it is only when we actually try to keep playing friendly football in the middle of a war that we discover we cannot. It is in action that we also discover these limits are indeed inevitable; that is, they are not just to do with personal weaknesses of will or lack of imagination, they are also a consequence of our finitude, our limited reach in a world structured by time and space. In other words, to stay with the metaphor, no one could have guaranteed actually reaching the generals and politicians to stop the War, let alone persuade them, even if we had an iron will, perfect judgement and total integrity. This world, structured as it is by the immense and complex interrelation of space and time, is just too dense to be fully penetrated by any one finite agent wishing to reshape it. Compromise with our ideals then becomes inevitable.

This is exactly what Bernard Williams found when he tried to implement socialist ideals in practice. He described finding a world as just too 'densely occupied' to yield to his principles (and his criticism of political philosophers like Robert Nozick and John Rawls was precisely that they failed to see this intrinsic complexity of reality because they had not really tested their theories by action). There are examples on a larger scale too, only too ready to hand. For instance, only when the international community tried through the UN to act to secure peace in the Congo in 1960 did it realize the sheer density of issues involved there. More perennially, only when we act in the Middle East do all the layers of complexity there emerge. The dilemma is sharpened because we are naturally agents, not just commentators or contemplatives; that is, our attempts to make things happen are an essential ingredient of human existence and identity, not just a dispensable adjunct.

Another reason for the inevitable frustration, however, lies paradoxically in the fact that we are *not* just agents. We are also idea-makers, contemplatives: that is, we have a capacity to extrapolate from particular things, people and situations and create general ideas about them. And this too sets up inevitable conflicts and compromise, because no general idea we form can then perfectly match all particular instances that underlie it. Particulars by definition have unique elements about them that cannot be generalized.

For example, if we think our child is treated unjustly at school we will necessarily have drawn on a general idea of what justice is (derived from the way others are treated); yet we will also be seeing unique elements in our child's particular situation that do not match that general principle and that (we think) make our child an exception. So again, the need to compromise is an inevitable outcome. This was exactly our ethicist Hauerwas' dilemma. What was generally right about guns and their ownership conflicted with what seemed right about the particular issue of accepting ownership of this particular gun in these particular circumstances. But we cannot give up having general and universal ideas any more than we can give up being agents. General ideas are what free us from the prison of the present moment and enable us to think and act more widely; they are necessary for all good science, social organization and even art. So that is why the dilemma is inevitable. This way in which the world structures our thinking to be *both* universal and particular leads inescapably to compromise.

A third reason is simply that we are always in a changing world – and a world in a state of organic transition is, in Jaspers' words, a natural 'zone of tragedy'. That is because any organically changing world (as distinct from a world that changes by wholesale revolution) has to deal with the new alongside continuing aspects of the old order. We should welcome this since organic development by definition works with the best of the old and does not wholly displace it. But it does then inevitably bring conflict between the two. So this too poses the dilemma of compromise. Hauerwas again provides the example. The young man was in transition between his new world of Christian social ethics and traditional family values. His new ideals mattered, but he could also still see the old values contained something good. Some form of compromise then becomes inevitable. And this is not just a passing problem, a temporary friction in a necessary process towards some final Hegelian resolution. For as long as we inhabit time we inhabit change too, especially this sort of organic change.

On all these counts, then, the dilemma of compromise is inevitable. It arises because we have to both act and think within complex structures of time and change, and in these deep structures of reality ideal outcomes are just not always possible. As Jaspers points out, the double bind is that, as reflective people, we can also *see* this, which can make matters worse by paralysing us. We are in that sense caught in the same dilemma as Hamlet, whom Jaspers judges to be paralysed not so much by some culpable weakness of character or moral blindness but, ironically, by clear vision. Hamlet has simply seen the impossibilities of life so clearly that he cannot see the point even of trying. It is another aspect of the dilemma.

So there is the analysis. Values will collide, idealism will be frustrated, life is bound to be tragic; and this is not just because of weakness of will (or 'sin') but also because of the basic structures of reality that we obviously cannot change. And it is an analysis that, on its own, could leave us just having to accept that this is the way it is.

But Karl Jaspers did not leave it there. As indicated, he also felt compelled to go 'beyond tragedy'. Why? Precisely because this thwarted idealism still felt like a *dilemma*, not just a brute fact. That is to say, it is because idealism, or at least the regret of it, persists even when thwarted; it is because it cannot be just shrugged off even when its limits can be shown to be structurally inevitable in all these ways. That is what drives us to look beyond the tragedy it generates.

Jaspers saw this persistence at work, especially in the phenomenon of what he calls 'guiltless guilt': that is, feeling guilty about compromises even though we can see they are inevitable. He noted this in spades through his own background as psychiatrist and his practical concern for post-war guilt. So he pursued it. But not simply to find therapy for it; rather, to see what it implied. Where is it pointing? It cannot just be pointing to actual guilt – as if we really could reach as far as our eyes see but do not try hard enough – because the whole point is that we cannot. So this raises the question. Could this unease, which feels like guilt but is not, suggest something else altogether? Might it imply there is more to reality, some resolution beyond tragedy, after all, even though we cannot currently reach it? This, for Jaspers, is just what it does imply. The fact that so many find they cannot just shrug their shoulders when idealism fails points at least to the possibility of a reality radically beyond current experience.

The force of the 'cannot' in the sentence 'we cannot just shrug our shoulders' is vital here. It does not seem to be only psychological: that is, something to be dealt with just by therapy or by cultivating a more robust temperament. It appears to be a more fundamental philosophical 'cannot': that is, a sense that reality itself cannot be exhausted by the limits it seems to have set for itself, so there must be more to it. In other words, when Jaspers moved in his own life from psychiatry to philosophy he was signalling that the experiences he was encountering demanded a re-framing of reality, not just of our minds. This is not fantasizing about reality like Williamson, because it is not denying reality (it fully accepts the impossibilities of life that are there); but it is finding something in experience that demands we expand reality. So Jaspers proceeds accordingly. To fully account for the experiences of guiltless guilt and continually pressing ideals, he begins to imagine that reality must include dimensions beyond space, time, tragedy; that is, he imagines what is normally called a transcendent dimension. Only this accounts for such a persistent moral light of idealism that refuses to settle with the compromises of our temporal existence. Only this gives these ideals meaning even when they cannot currently be fulfilled. In fact, Jaspers' own substantive appeal to this transcendent realm is abstract and undefined and so perhaps, as such, unpersuasive. But it is notable, nonetheless. It is surely significant that he has been driven to these transcendent imaginings by the pressure of precisely this conundrum of thwarted idealism we are exploring. And it helps explain why I now want to turn to a theological perspective on the dilemma.

A turn to theology

Theology, after all, is exactly the attempt to give some shape and content to this under-defined sense of transcendence. This is not necessarily by giving the transcendent clear, conceptual content. The idea of God in theology remains almost as shrouded in conceptual mystery as Jaspers' abstract transcendence. However, theology can and does give it some real *narrative* content. That is, 'God' in theology opens up a world-view with a coherent, concrete, purposive story; a story in which the persisting reality of ideals, their inevitable compromise and the drive still to pursue them can all make more sense. It is a story that philosophical speculation about the 'good' or the 'ideal' on its own cannot really match.

This story is in essence very simple. It begins first, like any cosmological story of the universe, with a process of creation. The creation of this limited, finite world of time, change, contingency and complexity is described not simply as a product of randomness or brute fact; nor as all there is. Instead, it is intentionally and purposefully brought into being like this by a transcendent personal mind and will. This purpose is then unfolded in history especially through the narratives of the Judaeo-Christian tradition. And what we see there is that this world is in fact a theatre for displaying certain kinds of meaning that can only be generated within the limits of finitude, time and change. Meaning emerges as we try to act well within those limits, as we strain against them to realize as much of the ideal as we can, even though we cannot realize it all ('pressing on toward the goal of the upward call', as St Paul puts it (Phil. 3:14)). It is precisely in the interplay of trying to realize conflicting ideals within these limits that the richest moral and spiritual meanings of life emerge; namely, experiences of sacrificial love, purposive co-operative endeavour, compassion, faith, humility and courage.

The story also tells how God offers us help in this theatre of the spirit; not only by pressing these ideals on us through our conscience, but also by helping to draw us towards them with His/Her active spiritual presence (what we call grace); not coercively (which would override our freedom), not *making* progress happen in every event (life is palpably not all progress), but working creatively with us to bring some good meaning from our efforts even when compromised (what we call providence). All this is particularly luminous in the story of Christ, where we see to a unique degree the pull towards an ideal, how it can be lived out through a compromising set of political and natural realities that thwarted him but that also generated deep meanings of sacrificial love precisely in his struggles with them. In this pivotal story, especially in its mysterious narratives of resurrection and ascension, we also see most clearly that there really is a transcendent source for these ideals; that is, we see a 'place' beyond tragedy (which we call eternity) where they can and will all be fulfilled; a place from which our response to these ideals is constantly renewed.

To set the dilemma in this sort of overall story and world-view, in this way, will more fully account for the dilemma; it makes more sense of this persistence of thwarted ideals and it re-frames the dilemma more positively. By describing idealism as the mind and will of God, it confirms the values of idealism as nothing else can; yet also, by describing compromise as the task of reaching as far as we can within limits to stretch our moral and spiritual fibre, it gives moral value to compromise as well. In short, it describes the world in which both our ideals *and* compromises are equally tools of moral and spiritual meaning. It is a metaphysics of the world in which thwarted ideals now seem more a gift than a curse and so provides a world-view in which we need never sink into cynicism when they are thwarted.

A personal meaning in a wider story

So this brings me to this final question. What metaphysic of the soul will match this metaphysic of the world? That is, what sort of persons can and should we be in order to operate best, specifically in *this* sort of world?

More of this follows in the next two essays. But this much at least can be said here. On the one hand this is the kind of world in which we cannot expect to be the sort of pcoplc who always get things absolutcly right, in the sense of always being able to act consistently with absolute moral principles to produce ideal outcomes. There will always be contradictions when we try to implement our ideals in that way, as Williams and Isaiah Berlin in their different ways acknowledged and for all the reasons that Jaspers exposed. But then is that really the main point anyway? Instead, the point is surely to be able to hold conflicting ideals together in some way without losing grip on them. It is here that Hauerwas is particularly illuminating; because what we can do within this world-view is still try to hold all ideals together in our character and in a whole narrative. That is, we can with God's grace be people whose deepest *disposition* is always for peace, justice and honesty, in the story as a whole, even though these principles may sometimes conflict in particular actions and practice. And this is a disposition that will be well supported if we can draw on this sort of resource of faith; that is, if we can see ourselves set within the wider narrative of an overall divine purpose for the world and eternity, a narrative in which ideals are not just dispensable creations of our own mind but exist eternally in God, always waiting to be realized as far as possible so that the very struggles of conflict and compromise can be seen as part of this spiritual narrative.

Do people of such disposition, character and mindset ever really exist in public life? Cynics may doubt it. But it was not doubted, for example, by the second Secretary General of the United Nations, Dag Hammarskjöld. He saw it in others, and he lived it himself to an extraordinary degree. His biographer, Roger Lipsey, paints the picture clearly and compellingly. Hammarskjöld was someone who was able to keep pressing for just peace through some of the most intractable international issues in the Cold War period, in the Middle East, Europe and Central Africa (that is, the proxy wars in still chillingly familiar places of conflict: Gaza, Suez, East Europe, the Congo). And he was able to keep pressing through massive setbacks and personal vilification precisely because he had a disposition sustained by this wider world-view of faith, which enabled him to remain both realistic and yet also unwaveringly idealistic, a world-view in which anything in the world could be a theatre of moral and spiritual striving, a theatre of the spirit. So he spoke of a view of history that often seems to run its course beyond the reach of any individual or nation and of a world that we cannot mould 'as masters of a material thing'; yet also of a world that we can still influence when we see it as 'a thing of the Spirit' (see Lipsey 2013).

And this is what I am offering. A response to the conundrum of idealism and compromise that is an invitation to see the world as a 'thing of the Spirit', a theatre for the Spirit and, as such, a world that, even in its frustrations, presents the possibility of living both realistically and idealistically. It is not offered as a trump card, as though the poets, psychologists, politicians and philosophers have all produced their *modus vivendi* just to be outgunned by the theologians. It is not like that. Each digs at different levels and helps feed each other. But it is offered nonetheless as a view that can justifiably sustain us positively through the experience of compromised idealism, rather than letting that drip of constant compromise just be corrosive to our idealism.

MORALITY

*Exploring the Implications
of Moral Authority*

The world is inevitably compromising. This is not just because of our moral deficiencies: it is the way we and the world are structured; it is because we are only finite agents with an inevitably limited reach in a finite world structured by space, time and change. It is also because we are idea-makers who form general principles to understand the world but then find these cannot cover every particular situation so we have to compromise between our principles and the claims of the particular.

There are even deeper reasons why the world is like this. These limits of finitude, space and time are not just a product of random chance. They are an intended, created order that provides conditions for the world to become a theatre of the spirit. These limits are necessary for the expression of profound purposes, meanings and virtues, such as sacrificial love, deep co-operation, courage, compassion, faith and humility, which can only be generated in a world where we have to struggle to realize our ideals in the face of these limits. This in turn points to a transcendent dimension to reality. For as our ideals strain against their limits, their persistence and our deep dissatisfaction when they are thwarted implies there really 'must' be a resolution to be found somewhere, even if not in this life and this world. In Karl Jaspers' philosophy, this hint of transcendence is only a shadowy and undefined dimension. In the Christian faith, it has much more definition: *God* is the ultimate mover and resolution of it all. The narrative of Christ then shows the Spirit of this God at work: that is where we see most clearly the Spirit pressing His ideals through the compromises and limits of the human life of Christ, forging these deep virtues of the spirit in the process and then finally confirming there is indeed a resolution beyond, in those mysterious narratives of resurrection and ascension.

Re-framing reality in this metaphysical or religious way does not just offer a theoretical resolution, it also forms a practical disposition in us. It means we will be people who are realistic because we have accepted compromise is inevitable (rather than retreating into fantasy or false guilt); yet we will still be motivated, precisely because these ideals remain real in God and, as such, can remain real in our own deep dispositions even when thwarted in many of our actions and decisions.

Such was the overall argument of the previous essay. However, there was a large assumption behind it. That is the assumption that these unsatisfied ideals we experience really do have this sort of authority: that is, the sort of authority that requires a metaphysical or religious explanation. In other words, it is the assumption that moral ideals are not just trivial facts of human psychology or biology that some people have, much as they have a taste for chocolate or an occasional headache. Rather, they have a unique character that requires a different category of explanation altogether. I now want to explore this assumption. I want to do this partly just because no assumption should be exempt from examination, but also because digging deeper into this unique authority of moral ideals will, paradoxically, help us further with the dilemma of compromise: that is, our apparent failure to fully comply with these pressing ideals.

Some preliminaries first. Digging deeper to religious roots of morality does not mean that religious world-views are the only source of wisdom. Far from it. So here again I shall be drawing on philosophy and literature, as well as some theology. I should also make clear that digging deeper like this is not the only way of being morally serious. Of course not. The morally serious George Eliot offers a good example. Her background was not religious or metaphysical but a more empirical, pragmatic Victorian agnosticism. And out of that background she felt no great need to explore the absoluteness of the moral demand. She simply appealed to what is possible. For her, when 'our eyes can see further than our hands can reach', the experience requires only that we try to be faithful to what is possible in the circumstances. There is no great residue of dissatisfaction we need worry about if we cannot go further. All that matters, like the old mantra of politics, is just the art of the possible.

This is nicely illustrated in the oft-quoted final reflections of Eliot's *Middlemarch*. Writing about her heroine, Dorothea, she says, '[the] determining acts of her life were not *ideally* beautiful...[just] the mixed result of a young and noble impulse struggling amidst the conditions of an imperfect social state'. Yet this still resulted in 'fine issues...for the growing good of the world is partly dependent on unhistoric acts; and that things are not so ill with you and me as they might have been, is half owing to the number who [simply] lived faithfully a hidden life'. In other words, for Eliot (unlike the writers of tragedy) real morality is not just about the ideals of heroic or historic acts that aspire to meet some absolute metaphysical divine demand; it can settle just for what is possible within the ordinary frames of life, just for what will at least make things 'not so ill as they would have been' (Eliot 1965, p.896, first published 1871–2).

It is, I admit, tempting to settle for this. Why can we not de-toxify these ideals we feel pressing on us? Why do we have to see them as an absolute external authority that needs explanation? Why can we not see them only as useful fictions to help keep us going as far as we can? It is especially tempting for the naturally pragmatic Anglo Saxon temperament. Preachers and philosophers may worry it is not enough, but then we Brits have a good track record in ignoring both preachers and philosophers.

However, I *am* both a preacher and philosopher, and I cannot just leave it there! So what follows is an explanation of why I do think it is worth digging deeper. It is an attempt to explain why, if we really reflect on moral idealism, its unique nature will inexorably lead us beyond pragmatism to metaphysics and faith. And to this end here are three features of morality that lead in this direction.

From morality to metaphysics: three features of moral authority

There is first the extraordinary and ineradicable energy of the moral impulse; that is, the way it keeps resurfacing across all time, space and culture. I do not just mean its resurgence in fundamentalist cultures where there is strict uniformity about what is right and wrong, I also mean the huge moral energy in liberal societies where there is disagreement about what is right and wrong. For even here, I suggest, we never lose the sense *that* there is a right and wrong, and this matters, even though we cannot always agree *what* is right and wrong. The massive moral energy in France displayed in reaction to terrorist incidents, especially the massacre of the *Charlie Hebdo* journalists in 2015, springs to mind.

A particularly telling way to show how this basic moral energy persists, even in liberal societies with big areas of moral relativism, is to chart the way this moral energy gets displaced into new areas rather than just disappearing. Rather than being dissipated by relativism, moral energy reappears in issues like the quest for efficiency and accountability. So for example, when mistakes of inefficiency or negligence rather than malice are made at work or in public life, we find people's reactions are just as searing as if it *was* malice. Why? It is because these reactions to inefficiency actually have this displaced moral energy behind them. Put another way, if a culture of relativism means I am no longer sure what is morally right or wrong about sexual ethics or a just war, I simply attach my moral energy instead to lambasting some hapless call centre operator for the inefficiencies of their company. It is, incidentally, in this way that the process of displacement has spawned both the litigious society and the bureaucratic society. The main point, though, is this: such displacement demonstrates just how irrepressible our underlying moral energy is, which then begs this question: if it is so ineradicable just what is it? Where does it come from?

Second, there is the distinctive nature of this moral impulse. There is the fact it just cannot be wholly reduced to anything else. And this begs this same question. What then is it, and where does it come from?

To be sure, we can try to demystify it and explain it just as a product of social or natural conditioning, a merely socio-biological reality. It is easy to tell that sort of story. For example, our evolutionary origins drive us to survive; for that we must co-operate; co-operation requires a measure of self-sacrifice; and so what we have taken to be distinctive moral claims have actually derived only from survival and expediency, which means the whole moral sense is really just a disguised outcrop of our evolutionary needs. And that all sounds very plausible.

But it really does not wash. The word 'just' ('just' an evolutionary product) betrays the slippery nature of the argument and exposes its flaw: the flaw of what is often called the genetic fallacy. This is the error of thinking that we know the nature of the outcome of a process just from the nature of the process that produced it. In this case, it is the error of assuming that because evolutionary processes cause the outcome of a moral impulse, the moral sense is itself nothing but a disguised survival or expediency instinct. This simply does not follow. It would be like saying that because the biological means of conceiving a child do not in themselves require thought, feeling or love, the outcome produced (the child) itself can have no real capacity for thought, feeling or love, for these are only disguised forms of the biological processes. That is nonsense: of course, a child has capacity for personal thought and feeling, even if the processes producing the child were impersonal. The outcome is not the same as the process. In the same way, the meaning of the moral impulse itself is distinctively moral even if the socio-biological processes producing it are not.

This fact that our moral impulse is distinctive is clearest in moral extremes. When we encounter something obviously and utterly evil, like the gratuitous hurting of vulnerable young people or the monstrosities committed by ISIS, we are repelled with a weight of feeling that requires distinct categories and language; that is, we do not see these sorts of acts as just 'inexpedient', or 'impractical', but precisely as *wrong*, as *evil*. It is the same when we encounter heroically good acts, whether these are the heroic Christ-like lives and actions of a Mandela or the self-sacrificing heroic lives of many unknown carers up and down the country who have consistently subordinated their own needs to care for another. When we encounter such lives we are moved and attracted by them, rather like the way great beauty moves us, in a unique and distinct way. We do not see them just as a disguised form of expediency or social contract but as qualitatively different; that is, they really are morally *good*, not just expedient. So again, as such, this begs the question: how can we account for this? Where does this extraordinary and distinctive meaning come from?

The third telling feature of the moral impulse is its perfectionism. That is, its drive to transcend limits, what might be called the 'infinity' of its ideals. This has been usefully explored by another political philosopher Simon Critchley (2007). The fact that Critchley is an atheist makes his analysis here more compelling. It is notable that as an atheist, naturally wary of religion and metaphysics, he still finds in the moral impulse this quality of infinity, its persistent need to transcend limits. He actually describes it in much the same way as Martin Luther described the unique authority of conscience. Its push and pull is so infinite that it never seems satisfied. In his own words, it endlessly 'vivisects' us, cuts ever deeper. And it would not do this, he says, if it was just the pull of pragmatism: it does so only as a distinct call of moral perfection.

Let me make this concrete. Think for example of the dynamics of an encounter with someone who falls down in the street in front of us, one of the many homeless encountered daily on London streets. What we may experience is not just a limited contractual or reciprocal claim on us. It is potentially limitless. Superficially, the claim may seem limited (help him to his feet if you can) and implicitly contractual (someone might do the same for us one day). But in fact the sense of claim on us almost certainly goes deeper than that. Should I also check whether there is anyone to look after him? Should I take him to the hospital? And it can go even further. Through this particular person's plight, we may wonder about others as well. Should I begin to work for a wider social justice to help all other claimants? Maybe he is an ex-serviceman whom we did not collectively help enough when he returned damaged from a war we sent him to. So what should I do about that too? In short, this claim can indeed feel infinite. It is something Critchley can only describe as a 'God-like' claim: that is, it is like meeting universal ideals and responsibilities that could only belong to a God. Critchley does not believe in God, yet in this infinite nature of moral idealism that we experience he feels that he has to reach (like Plato and Kant before him) for quasi-religious language to express it. So once again it begs the question: how do we account for such a transcendent phenomenon?

It is a question that demands a whole-world view by way of a response. And I will come to that shortly.

First, however, just this clarification. What if – more like George Eliot than Plato or Kant – we simply do not experience the moral impulse to be like this? What if this moral call simply does not feel like an infinite burden always pressing on us? Does it invalidate the implications I want to draw from it? Or, indeed, is it a sign of some moral deficiency in us?

Neither! In fact I suspect that most of us actually feel relatively little moral weight in day-to-day routine acts and decisions, whether in public service or private life. Our routine moral 'feeling' is quite likely to be little different from the sort of feeling we have about what we had for lunch: that is, we may be generally nourished by an underlying sense of right and wrong but hardly overwhelmed by the taste of it all the time; we are not routinely sensing morality as this unique, intense, authoritative, infinite demand compelling us to metaphysical reflection. Put another way, we are not all Hamlets, Lears, Othellos, Antigones, constantly torn with tragic moral angst. We are mostly operating more like Shakespeare's wise fools, getting on with reality more pragmatically, to move things on to the next scene. And if so, thank God. No one can live all the time with too much intensity, and it certainly should not be considered a moral deficiency.

But is this absence of moral intensity in routine experience relevant for the meaning of morality itself? Surely not. It is not evidence that we *never* experience deep moral feeling. And what matters for the meaning of morality (and our own moral authenticity) arises much more clearly from extreme situations of good or evil, where our reaction *is* likely to be intense, and that is what will really press the questions I want to pursue. What then *is* the ultimate nature and meaning of this profound moral reaction?

From metaphysics to God

The response to this I will now propose is simple and perhaps unsurprising. But I believe it is compelling. What we are encountering in this unfulfillable moral ideal with its unique authority is what even Critchley found himself half-driven to, in spite of himself. That is, we are meeting the mind and will of a personal God. For there is an intimate and natural connection specifically between moral sense and religious sense. In fact, in my view, it is the most enduring and convincing of all the classic bridges between general human experience and God.

Why? It is because the push and pull of moral impulse is precisely like meeting a personal will. It is at least like meeting another human mind and will, particularly that of a powerful and attractive personality. To encounter this sort of person is to feel their mind, will and desires impinging on us in almost exactly the way a strong moral claim does: that is, it pushes us away from things they do not want and pulls us towards things they do want. And so if we then experience this same push and pull of conscience in a uniquely energetic, authoritative, infinite form (which, as such, could not be just a human voice) it becomes natural to see it as the will of a personal God. This does not mean that we always experience the *content* of the divine will reliably in our conscience. Of course not. This moral impulse is always mediated, and distorted, by our flawed humanity and surrounding culture. That is why there is moral disagreement. But the *form* of the moral impulse remains God-like, whatever the flaws of its content, for all the reasons suggested. And this, I suggest, is a much more compelling account of it than describing it as a purely socio-biological instinct.

To be sure, we may be embarrassed to name it as such. We may even be embarrassed to own it just as a strong moral sense, let alone as a sense of God. If so, we would not be alone. Ernest Hemingway in *For Whom the Bell Tolls* (1940) wrote that his moral feeling of 'consecration to a duty toward all of the oppressed of the world' was 'as difficult and embarrassing to speak about as a religious experience'. But the fact remains he had that strong sense, and the fact also remains that it is at least an eloquent metaphor of the mind of God. So if we are in the business of nourishing the moral and spiritual resources of our public discourse and action, we may have to overcome this embarrassment. Giving explicit voice and language to these underlying realities that shape us is key to this task.

Religious morality, human responsibility and motivation

But what *practical* difference does it make if we give the moral impulse this explicit metaphysical or religious location? And in particular, what does a religious underpinning add to our practical experience of actually living with impossible moral ideals and with the compromises they inevitably bring?

First, paradoxically, I believe it can provide us with a huge and proper sense of release. It is paradoxical because naming a moral impulse as divine might seem only to crush us under a weight of perfectionism. But, in fact, it is the opposite, because it can at least provide release from a sense of ultimate responsibility. After all, if this impulse to perfection, this sense of infinite, universal responsibility represented by moral sense, comes ultimately from God, not just our own minds or from society, then of course we cannot be finally responsible for fulfilling it. How can we be finally responsible for what we have not created?

This echoes the point made in the previous essay. As finite creatures there are inevitable limits both to our reach and our responsibility. To some extent we may think we know these limits anyway, regardless of any wider religious world-view. Just by living longer and growing older we have come to know better the dependencies and limits imposed on us by our genes, our upbringing and our culture in a way we never fully realized when we were younger. But to know ourselves specifically as creatures of God, not just of our parents and culture, makes this dependency even more radical. So it should also make the release greater from the angst of thinking *we* can ever achieve it all. It should free us once and for all from the myth of the doctrine of inevitable human progress, the myth of rationalism and scientific socialism that we alone could eventually meet all our ideals, individually or collectively. A theistic world-view, at best, should release us from all this and should form in us instead a deeper wisdom: that is, a character and fundamental disposition that is less arrogant, more realistic.

Another, related, form of release it should bring is to free us from an over-tragic response to our limits and failed ideals. What I mean by this is the temptation, when we fail to meet all our ideals, to find satisfaction instead in a sense of heroic failure. It is the temptation to paint ourselves proudly as victims of forces beyond our control that we at least tried to conquer, even though we inevitably failed. It is a temptation because this sort of reaction to compromise or failure just deflects our efforts into portraying ourselves with this heroic sense of self-justification rather than continuing to pursue the real goal of our original endeavour more realistically in some other way.

Examples of this from political rhetoric, from left and right, easily present themselves. From the left, consider some of the rhetoric of the miners' strike in the 1980s; from the right, rhetoric about Europe at the time of the election of a new European Commission president. In both cases protagonists aimed at a sincerely perceived good. In the first case, the aim was to secure benefits for miners in relation to impending pit closures. In the second, the aim was to benefit the British people in relation to impending European hegemony. In both cases, when each of these conflicted with other goals of the time and their goal was not secured (that is, survival of the pits and major concessions from Europe), there was then inevitable compromise or failure. A familiar set of circumstances. But the point here lies in the way that failure was then represented by the protagonists. In both cases, there was a notable tendency to represent it by heroic tragedy; that is, by protagonists representing themselves as going down fighting righteously. This displaced effort from achieving at least something of their original good goal in other ways. Another example was a previous government's reaction to the long-term failure of the invasion of Iraq. All the same dynamics were there: a leader casting himself in a heroic mould to draw attention to his own integrity, but his very sense of rightness was tending to deflect further constructive efforts to pursue the cause in another way.

The overall point, then, is simply that a deep recognition that the ultimate origin and responsibility for all true ideals is not ourselves but the mind of God renders this sort of tragic self-regarding response ridiculous. So it frees us as nothing else can from the fantasy that *we* always have to be seen to succeed. And it should, again, form us with a disposition and character that is more realistic, relaxed and humble.

Finally, there is also the practical implication of re-motivating us when we do fail. A religious frame clearly helps here too. Why? Because even as it helps us see our limits and failures as inevitable, it should also help us see them as redeemable. And that can re-energize us. For if we see these pressing ideals not just as an abstract moral or social demand but also as the will of a personal God, relating to us personally, a wholly different reaction to our inevitable compromises and failures becomes more possible. An abstract cause or ideal cannot support us, nor can it forgive when we fail. It can only condemn. But a personal God can support and forgive. S/He can pick us up and keep us pressing forward, rather than withdrawing, giving up or, worse, fantasizing heroically. *Prima facie* this could seem the opposite of a release from the angst of striving. But in fact it just reveals the real practical genius of this religious world-view; in the face of thwarted ideals and sense of moral failure it can combine both a sense of release and continued motivation.

Does anyone, can anyone, really live like this in public life? Are people in public life ever so deeply formed in a religious disposition as this? 'Doing God' in public life is rarely admitted. But again I want to offer as an exemplar the same figure cited in the previous essay: Dag Hammarskjöld, the second Secretary General of the United Nations. He never paraded his faith, but it is nonetheless clear from his diary and letters that he was deeply formed in character and dispositions by a rich inner life of spiritual reflection. He frequently drew deeply on the religious nature of the ideals he held; a spirituality and theology based chiefly in a Christian

Lutheran upbringing, but also drawn from Christian mystics, Jewish and eastern spiritualities.

What is particularly clear is the way he experienced this personal divine will not as a series of abstract edicts and principles that could all be perfectly kept, but precisely as the experience of a personal will who could and would continually inspire him through a long narrative of trying, failing and trying again. So that what Hammarskjöld thought he was doing was not just trying to carry out abstract principles; it was not an examination in ethical mathematics (making principles add up that just do not in this world); instead, he was experiencing the moral impulse precisely as if it was a person supporting him, forming his character over time, forgiving and restoring him.

As such, Hammarskjöld never saw himself as anything more than just one partner with God in projects that he knew he alone would never solve. This meant he could always trust that God would pick up the pieces through others, where he himself fell short. And that is what motivated him. That is the full measure of what summoned him to enter the minefields of Gaza, Suez, the Congo crisis and Cold War tensions and what sustained him purposively, even when exhausted and vilified. Abstract principles of justice, democracy and freedom were not sufficient. It was this sense of summons and support within a personal relationship with God that kept motivating him without becoming cynical, fantasizing or retreating to self-aggrandizement. Such a sense of a realistic, humble yet motivated partnership with God and others is captured in many fragments from his letters and diary. All that matters, he believed, was the slow and collective effort of many towards the goal, and our own capacity 'to vanish as an end and remain purely as a means' (Lipsey 2013, p.543). It is a long way from heroic posturing!

My argument, therefore, has been this. First, to establish that this assumption that there are real, pressing ideals is defensible: the moral impulse cannot be deconstructed into something less real and less pressing; it does have a unique character and authority. Second, to suggest this impulse, as such, only really makes full sense within a religious metaphysic and to acknowledge that explicitly. Finally, to say more about a matching metaphysic of the soul that should be formed in us: that is, a personal character and disposition that will be both realistic and yet always able still to press forward, even when 'our eyes can see further than our hands can reach'...

PURPOSEFULNESS

Exploring the Implications of Our
Pervasive Sense of Purpose

Our eyes see further than our hands can reach. That is, we have ideals but cannot fulfil them. This common experience, in both public and private life, is not trivial. It matters to us. For philosopher Karl Jaspers it is the heart of all tragedy. And in the previous essays I have explored the conundrum it creates in two ways: I have suggested it is inevitable (given our finite reach in this complexly structured world); I have also suggested it is ineradicable (in the sense that the moral impulse that drives our ideals has a unique and absolute authority that will not reduce just to contingent socio-biological factors). This last point is, in turn, suggestive. It seems to beg a religious or metaphysical origin to make sense of it. It invites us to look for a wider and deeper spiritual narrative in which to locate ourselves; that is, one that enables us to keep pursuing our ideals purposefully and with integrity in this compromising world – and that sustains us even when we (inevitably) fail to realize them all.

So this now brings me to explore more fully this further ingredient of the conundrum: that is, the extraordinary persistence not just of moral ideals but also of our sense of *purpose* in this compromising world. How is it that we do and can retain purposefulness even when our hands so often fail to reach what our eyes can see? And what does this imply about the nature of the world and ourselves?

To pursue this, I will first briefly explain what I mean by our sense of purpose and then show just how extraordinarily persistent and pervasive it is throughout history, even when there is no progress in history. Then, as with the moral impulse in the previous essay, I will suggest what this implies: that is, how naturally this experience of persistent purpose sits within a wider world-view of faith. Finally, I will suggest what sort of personal character this implies for us: what kind of people we need to be to sustain such purposefulness realistically.

First, then, the preliminary point: what do I mean by a sense of purpose? I mean simply the sense that we are all part of a story with a role to play and a goal to reach; and, crucially, the sense that we have not entirely created this story ourselves, that is, the story and goal are partly given, not just invented. This sense is, I believe, deeply embedded in our culture and psychology. Like the moral impulse, it does not depend on any conscious religious allegiance. It is more widespread than that. It appears for many simply part of the grain of reality. There just *is* this sense of teleology, the pull towards a given goal and purpose, of some sort. And it certainly underlies the conundrum of thwarted idealism.

It is not an uncontroversial definition. The alternative, of course, is that our sense of purpose, far from being about something objective, is indeed entirely something we have made up to give ourselves meaning. That is the view of one of the most vocal critics of any real objective purpose, Richard Dawkins, who thinks that we are just inveterate storytellers;

that is, we are just natural inventors of meaning, not finders of a meaning that is really there.

Yet does our natural propensity to invent meaning actually imply what Dawkins supposes? Is it not just as likely, perhaps more likely, that the instinct to create meaning is actually a response to something really there? That, after all, is the case with most of our other most basic human instincts, which in fact are usually signs that there is something really there to satisfy them. For example, we are hungry for food because there really is such a thing as food. Or we long for love because there really are such things as satisfying human relationships. So why should our instinct for a story be any different? Perhaps we instinctively invent stories about the purposes of life because in fact there really is an objective purpose there to be found.

T. S. Eliot illustrates this tellingly in his poem 'Gerontion'. The old man of 'Gerontion' certainly invents. He looks back sentimentally on life, trying to make sense of it by creating a story for it, not least to cast himself in a better light. In that sense his story is just an invention, self-deceiving ('think now, history has many cunning passages, contrived corridors... deceives with whispering ambitions, guides us by vanities'). But then why does it matter to him so much to do this? Because deep down he knows there is actually a real story to be told as well, even if it is not the one he is inventing: he has to discover '*The* Word' within our own words (Eliot 1969, first published 1920, emphasis mine).

That, then, is what I mean by our sense of purpose: a core instinct that we are part of an objective story, which is a given, not just invented, purpose in life. What I now want to do is also show briefly just how embedded and persistent it is through western history, not just in our individual psyches;

how it is so rooted in us that it persists in some form through so many different cultural and intellectual contexts (see White 2015 *Purpose and Providence* for a fuller account).

Philosophy, church and society: the persistence of purpose through history

For example, we can readily trace it in classical philosophy in Aristotle with his hugely influential teleological analysis of reality, his view that all things naturally tend towards given goals and end purposes. Or we could begin even further back in classical culture with Euripides and the Stoics and their equally dominating sense of overall order: a natural order of justice and cosmic necessity, presided over by the gods, to which all things must inevitably conform because it was their purpose, their fate. Later we can see Spinoza operating with something similar with his Christianized sense of overall cosmic order. And later still there has been the turn to history as a determination to see purpose above all in temporal 'progress': that is, in the supposed movement to an ever-better life in the history of this world, a historicized view of purpose that peaked in the great nineteenth-century philosophical and theological traditions of Hegel and Marx. In all these eras some sense of real objective purpose has undoubtedly persisted, with or without explicit appeal to God.

What is more, this sense of purpose has persisted even when the supposed supporting evidence of progress has crumbled. In both church history and political history progress itself has foundered as a doctrine. For the church, the seminal recognition of this goes back to Augustine. In the patristic age, when God's master plan for the church was first thought of as a straight linear sequence of visible success and acceptance, it seemed natural to interpret events like the conversion of the emperor Constantine and the cessation of martyrdom as evidence that this progress was really happening. But in fact, almost from the beginning, Augustine saw how facile this was and warned against it. Rightly so. Constantinianism, where the church assumed worldly power, did not prove an unqualified success. With the subsequent fall of Rome, schism between east and west, the Reformation and Enlightenment, this became even clearer: the church was not evidently progressing in any obvious straight line but often fracturing and declining. The various nineteenth-century European plans of progress for the church suffered similar setbacks. No simple linear progress happened. The pressure of real events saw to it. Church mission faltered with the rise of pluralism and global consumerism. The doctrine of an inevitably unfolding Kingdom of God on earth foundered in the horror of the First World War. And for secular social and political history a similar story can be told. Social philosopher John Gray is uncompromising about the failures of all secular programmes when predicated on an ideology of progress (e.g. Gray 2007). He cites examples from Marxism to unfettered capitalism, to liberal interventionism. Each has eventually failed, even in its own terms, inviting disillusionment. Each has been discredited not least when it has turned to various forms of instrumental coercion to try to achieve the success when thwarted.

However – and here is the point – a sense of purpose has still persisted, in both church and political world, even when progress has palpably failed in all these ways. The church still keeps trying to embody the Kingdom of God, regardless of the dismal lessons of some of its history. Governments still keep trying to reform education, health, national security, the environment or even the national happiness quotient. These remain as goals and purposes, even when a measure of failure keeps subverting those efforts. That is why we try new paths, duck and weave, swing from centralized control to localism, and back again, from colonialism to isolationism to liberal interventionism, and back again. Even when none of these ploys lastingly produces progress we still pursue our goals as if they are real and possible because the residual power of purpose is never wholly snuffed out.

In short, whether in personal experience or the experience of institutions and nations, purposiveness endures. The sad old man fantasizing in Eliot's 'Gerontion', the visionary teenager following a dream to become a celebrity or join Jihadists, the political body creating its manifesto, all embody this deep instinct to persist with some sense of purpose as if we are pursuing something real, whether or not we succeed. As with the inexorable pull of moral ideals I explored in the last essay, purpose keeps pulling us forward, regardless of success or compromise. It is an extraordinary persistence that, I suggest, reinforces the initial definition I proposed: that is, our purposiveness is a sign of something really there to be found, not just an invention of our wishful thinking.

Finding purpose even in the sceptics

Because this is so important to establish (not least in the face of an equal persistence of scepticism about it) let me also now 'stress test' it even further. That is, I want to try to demonstrate this objectivity of purpose even in contexts where it is most questioned; I want to try to show its persistence even where ultimate order and purpose is systematically doubted and deconstructed, and randomness rules. For if we even find it in our doubts, if we find we have to doubt our doubt, then it must indeed be reckoned with...

So, for example, it can be tested out in the thought of Dawkins' own mentor, in Darwin himself. His theory of evolution certainly denied any objective intentionality and purpose in things; it suggested instead that the processes of evolution occur in theory by random natural selections shaped only by the exigencies of environment and survival, not by any other external directing purpose. But, in fact, if you read *The Origin of Species* and look carefully at the language that Darwin uses, you will encounter an extraordinary feature: it actually breathes purpose through every pore. The apparently random process of evolution is described in a narrative as a purposive *story*; it is a scientific account, certainly, but written precisely as a story and as if it has an author. As one commentator has put it, it is written as 'Darwin's *Plots*', the title of a brilliant exposition by literary critic Gillian Beer (2000). Darwin himself actually admits this at one point. In the third edition of *The Origin of Species* he denies that his theory necessarily means any sort of external hand is at work to give purpose, but he does admit that the nature of the processes he is describing still seem to breathe this story-like quality, *as if* they are not just random.

I have also tested this instinct out in sceptical, post-Darwin literary observers of life: that is, those who write self-consciously as post-Christian, post-metaphysical thinkers. To trawl the writings of many whose assumption is of a purpose*less* world is to find that, despite themselves, they reveal cracks in this apparently random, purposeless reality they set out to describe; cracks through which traces of a sense of purpose keeps appearing. One example is late nineteenth-century poet and novelist Thomas Hardy. Purpose haunts his work throughout even though he frequently describes a much more Darwinian world-view. Perhaps this is to be expected in someone originally formed in childhood in classical and Christian teleology who might simply be reflecting lingering traces of his childhood beliefs. But then I also find the same in another example, in the contemporary post-modern novelist Julian Barnes, who never had a faith in God or purpose to lose. And since Barnes is more radical, his example is even more telling.

There is no doubt, to begin with, that he generally finds the world to be purposeless. It is perhaps most explicit in *A History of the World in 10½ Chapters* (Barnes 2009, first published 1989). Here the whole structure is designed to make the point. For what he calls a history is in fact ten different, short, separate stories, which, apart from a few very loose thematic connections, are deliberately disparate; there is no chronological sequence to link them and no obvious causal connection between each – no overarching purpose at all. It is summed up in one chapter about a nineteenth-century expedition to discover Noah's Ark on Mount Ararat, where one of the characters looks for 'a divine intent, benevolent order and justice', but all that he sees is 'chaos, hazard and malice'. The final summary statement of a narrator is even starker, 'Our current model for the universe is [just] entropy, which at the daily level translates [simply] as: things fuck up'. It is much the same when he looks at the history of a personal life in a later novel *The Sense of an Ending* (Barnes 2011). Like Eliot's old man in 'Gerontion', he is someone who wants to make or find sense of his life, but he cannot. His honesty will not let him. All he actually sees in his life, we are told on the final page, is only random accumulation of experience, just 'unrest...great unrest'.

Yet – and this again is the point – even here if you look carefully there are still signs of purpose. Even when he has tried to strip his world-view of what he sees as false religion, false superstition and false ideology, even though repeated evidence from history and his own life suggest that the world is just random, even then his novels still show signs of purpose. It seems that same rigorous honesty that makes Barnes record the apparent randomness of the world as the dominant 'narrative' has also required him to record signs of purpose as well – against the grain.

So, for example, in that apparently purposeless structure of the *History of the World in 10½ Chapters*, there is actually an underlying link after all. To look closely at the opening story, which is an ironic mimicry of the Noah's Ark story as the beginning of world history, is to see that in fact this sets up a link with the other stories. For there is one survivor of the ark, a narrator, who does keep reappearing. It is easy to miss. It is only a woodworm, a parasite, that has survived. But it is there nonetheless, worming its way through the various other disparate tales, feeding off everything that happens: a hint that purpose *can* be found in everything after all?

Moreover, in one chapter (the half of the 10½!) Barnes suddenly becomes the narrator himself, interrupts the whole history and gives a strange but impassioned discourse on love. However meaningless and random things are, he says, we must keep believing in the purpose of love. 'Must'? This 'must' is curious. It is expressed with the force of metaphysical, not just psychological, necessity. It is as if the force of love we feel is not just one more random thing but does have objective meaning and purpose, even when events only seem, as he says, to 'fuck things up'. Again, is this a hint of some objective purpose after all? It echoes, incidentally, a telling moment in a seminar for army officers on leadership and motivation by Westminster Abbey Institute. A serving officer described how a sense of purpose can persist in soldiers even in extreme circumstances of total chaos. It was not, he said, just because of discipline or training. It was because of love: love of comrade, even if not of the cause; and it was a purpose of love so real, compelling and 'different' that he could only describe it as a 'spiritual thing'.

In short, even in the science of Darwin, in the scepticism of literary post-modernism – and for that matter in the extremities of a battlefield – a sense of objective purpose is still there to be found. There is always a hidden worm of meaning, a purpose of love, this spiritual thing, burrowing behind the scenes. To be sure, from time to time we can and do all lose this sense of purpose; we can lose belief in it and the motivation to find it. That is a form of depression, individual or collective, from which I suspect we all can suffer from time to time and which any honest look at the world surely comprehends. Yet even so, the default setting, the underlying reality that I am trying to describe, is still there; there *is* always purpose to be found, even in chaos.

Where purpose leads us: a sense of purpose in the wider narrative of life

So the final question follows inexorably. Given such extraordinary, pervasive, persistent purposefulness: what does it *mean* about the world and ourselves? What does it imply? It is the same sort of question I have employed throughout these essays and the same form of argument. Having identified an irreducible feature of human experience – first our ideals, then our basic moral impulse and now our sense of purpose – I want to suggest that there are inescapable implications. I want to suggest that the unique personal nature and persistence of these experiences, even in the face of a compromising and apparently random world, cries out for an explanation. In fact, it actually requires a whole metaphysic to account for them, one that goes beyond the minimalist explanations either of bare fate or mere scientism.

Thus, in this case of purpose, it will not be adequately explained as the ancients did, just as impersonal fate, nor as some scientism does just as impersonal random mechanisms of evolution. For neither of these account for the personal nature of this persistent pull of purpose on us, the way in which it always engages our personal aspirations and often comes to us as the call of love. But what *will* make sense of that, however, is to see it within a metaphysic of faith: that is, when we see the irrepressible pull of purpose quite simply as the pull of a personal God and His or Her purposes, of love; a transcendent God whose pull through this difficult, compromising world persists precisely because it is not created just by us but comes from a reality who can finally fulfil it beyond time and chance.

Our sense of purpose sits naturally within that interpretation, because the specific ways the Judaeo-Christian tradition has portrayed God's purpose at work matches that general sense of purpose so well in the ways I have been describing. In particular, it matches a purpose that persists without requiring visible progress. God's purpose in scriptural narrative, after all, is not represented just as linear progression to a final overall fulfilment at the end of the whole process; instead, it is represented in particular moments that only surface sporadically throughout a chequered history of ups and downs, a history of compromises and failures. So, for example, God's promises to Israel are fulfilled only through 4000 years so far of devastating trials and triumphs, wilderness wanderings, exile, homecoming, diaspora, near genocide and back to homeland again (who knows what next?). Likewise, the promises of God to the Christian Church have been operating through a very chequered 2000-year history that has followed a similar pattern, just as Augustine foresaw. There was first a great expansion of Christian faith in the ancient world, but then divisions, retreat in the Enlightenment and Industrial Revolution, at least in Europe, and then growth again, at least elsewhere in the world; but again, who knows what next? It is within and through all that patchwork of repeated crosses and resurrections, not through smooth linear progress, that God's purpose calls. It is a purpose fulfilled in particular struggles of faith, love and hope forged along that same chequered path, not just in the end result (efforts of faith and love that can be held in eternity whether or not they reach any visible fulfilment in history).

It is this same biblical pattern, I suggest, that will make sense of our secular histories too, not just our religious history. This is the pattern that can make sense of all continuing private and political purposive efforts for good personal relationships, or for social justice, even though we may end our life without seeing the outcome we hoped for at some linear end point. It is when they are seen as part of a divine purpose that can give them eternal value in themselves that they gain a sense and credibility, rather than locating them in any utopian dream or secular ideology that requires some successful end point in time. Put simply, it means that if you or I or a political programme end up in time in tatters (as we all do), that does not ultimately matter; it does not undermine their final purpose. For all that was good and worthwhile in particular moments on the way still has meaning as part of the wider divine purpose in time and eternity.

Here we also see how practically transforming this world-view can be, particularly in its power to motivate. After all, to believe that particular actions can have this depth of meaning and purpose in this way in themselves, even when thwarted in the linear passage of time, can keep us motivated in frustrating times as nothing else can. This motivating power is visible in human relationships whenever we see people instinctively engage in individual acts of generosity with other people (including strangers) without needing to see that action validated by some visible long-term outcome. It can be seen in other contexts too. In a political context it means, for example, that we can see the worthwhileness of full democratic rights and freedoms in our own particular situation, and be willing to defend them, without needing to see that value depending on their long-term success universally. This is, surely, an important lesson for the west to learn in geopolitics, where too often our sense of moral purposiveness has depended on feeling we have to see it and enforce it beyond our own particular context as well. And the point is, it is the perspective of faith that helps cement this overall disposition: for it is *sub specie aeternitatis* that we never have to justify the purpose of some particular project by reference just to an overall final success we see in time.

In this way, we also surely see again the sort of people we shall need to be within this sort of world. We see a metaphysic of the soul to match our metaphysic of the world. That is, we see that we shall need to be the kind of people whose deepest disposition is to keep acting purposefully in particular situations without needing visible success and without feeling we have to make everything successful by coercion. We see we shall need to be people with enduring hope and motivation in everything, yet always yoked with humility, realism and respect for what has to be left outside our remit (that is, left to God working through others and in eternity).

It is Dag Hammarskjöld who again serves as a real-life exemplar of this disposition. At a gathering of the press corps of the UN General Assembly, on 9 April 1958, after struggling with both monumental successes and setbacks in Suez, China and the wider Middle East, he is on record as saying 'Very often I ask myself...have we made progress?' Implicitly he answers no, not in any empirical visible sense, for as his biographer makes clear (Lipsey 2013), he did not subscribe to any facile faith of previous generations that progress was inevitable. Even so, he was confident that with certain kinds of people the future can be good: but only those kinds of people who do not have pretensions to make everything happen themselves and who are willing to be 'only a means and not an end'. In short, people who can still live purposefully even when idealism is frustrated; people who, when their 'eyes see further than [their] hands can reach' will not retreat to either fantasy, coercion or cynicism, yet will still be able to sustain a realistic pursuit of ideals.

Such is the disposition, in public and private life, that can sustain ideals, morality and purpose in a compromising world. And this is a disposition that, as I have tried to show, will itself be sustained credibly and aptly if we are also prepared to live within this wider world-view of faith. People of this disposition but without faith also exist of course. But it is equally certain this faith can help make a unique sense of it.

The Staying Power of Benedict in Parliament Square

Rowan Williams

Introduction: Charles Gore's community and Benedictine stability

This essay is based upon the Charles Gore Lecture I gave at Westminster Abbey in 2016. Charles Gore is remembered, among other things, for founding the Community of the Resurrection, which still thrives in Mirfield, Yorkshire. This community was not, and is not, primarily a Benedictine foundation. Many other elements of monastic traditions played their part in defining the ethos of the Mirfield community. But one element in its life is held in common with all monastic traditions, and it is that element which is perhaps the most central element in Benedictine identity: *stability*. *The Rule of Benedict* (Benedict 2016, first published in the sixth century CE) is, in one sense, all about stability; that is to say that it is all about staying in the same place, with the same people. The height of self-denial, the extreme of asceticism, is not hair shirts and all-night vigils; it is standing next to the same person in choir and sitting next to them in refectory for years on end. So when St Benedict attempts to spell out in one of the early chapters (Chapter 4 of the Rule) what he calls 'The Tools of Good Works', all of these 72 'Tools' have to be understood in the context of this summons to stability. Stability, for Benedict, is the condition for learning about the human, the background against which we develop who we are as human agents, because at its basis lies the recognition that others are not going to go away or stop being other. A great deal of our politics, our ecclesiastical life, often our personal life as well, is dominated by the assumption that everything would be all right if only some people would go away. We see this in our national life in our attitudes both to Europe and to migrants, and there is a great deal more to be said about that in other contexts. But the point is that, for the writer of the Rule of Benedict, other people are *not* going to go away; and therefore the heart of the spiritual challenge is how we live with that continuing, obstinate otherness: honestly, constructively, hopefully and not blindly.

Not going away

The recognition that others will not go away is of spiritual importance because it is also a recognition that I am always going to be faced with what is not me and not under my control. My spiritual quest is how I live with this without resentment or lying, without despair, with clarity and without 'abjection' before the other, being enslaved by the other. How do I develop an adequate strategy of living with that strangeness around me? Others are no more there on sufferance than I am *here* on sufferance. And so the Tools of Good Works in Chapter 4 of the Rule could be interpreted as a whole raft of ways of creating and maintaining an environment that nourishes us in the growth of the skills we need in living with the stranger.

The Tools of Good Works as spelled out by Benedict include a great many of what you might call routine community virtues: the corporal works of mercy, the golden rule and quite a few of the Ten Commandments. In other words, the Tools of Good Works are, like so much written by Benedict, very prosaic affairs. But you can read the Tools of Good Works chapter as spelling out what it is like to live in a way that creates an environment that is *dependable*: an environment that has continuity about it, such that it is possible for people to grow, an environment such that you are not constantly seeking to make up a definition of yourself out of whole cloth. Benedict is asking what it takes to develop people who can live safely, consistently and positively together. So he does not write the Rule beginning with a recommendation of stability as an abstract idea; he tries to outline an environment where the long-term sameness of my company will not breed bitterness, cynicism or fear of openness among them. If you do have to spend a lifetime with the same people, it is certainly possible without too much difficulty to create a set of strategies to manage this fairly successfully, but strategies of managing it will create the exact opposite of the sort of openness towards which Benedict is working, unless they are grounded in the recognition of our limits, of the inescapable out-of-controlness of others and of the possibility of finding grace and gift in this.

Honesty, peace, accountability

When we list the content of the Tools, we can very broadly list Benedict's recommendations under three headings. He wants his community to be: an environment of *honesty*; an environment of *peace*; and an environment of *accountability*. Honesty, peace and accountability are the conditions in which stability flourishes: honesty, because you can depend on the other to tell you the truth systematically; peace because you need to know that the basis of your shared life is not a matter of constant and insecure negotiation with others; accountability because you need to know who is responsible for what and how that responsibility works. Now, as you may have noticed, not a huge number of people join Benedictine monasteries; they are after all voluntary associations, as are all religious communities. So we always have the challenge of working out exactly how to recommend it to the society around, how to persuade people voluntarily to share its vision. Monastic life, like Christian life overall, is a form of life that depends on people having chosen it. It makes an offer, a proposal, to its society. *What if* this kind of life were possible after all? That is what the church, the monastery and many other kinds of intentional community are trying to say. What if stability, honesty and so on were indeed for all of us, not just for a few, the basis of human life together? And it is the testimony represented so powerfully by the presence of Westminster Abbey in Parliament Square that embodies this proposal: an offer, a presence that speaks not just of the royal and national traditions so richly in evidence all around us, but also of a tradition rather more deep and more critical that has to do with the fundamental possibilities of stability and its spiritual fruits: of how to work with stability in honesty, in peacefulness and in accountability. And – not to labour the point too much – that is why the believing community, whether the monastery in particular or the church in general, is so deeply self-wounded when it fails in honesty, peacefulness and accountability. All of us, I dare say, have stories about those failures, how very public and conspicuous they can be and how very lethal for church and society.

Honesty

A few words, then, about how Benedict actually treats these specifics, in his discussion of the Tools of Good Works. Honesty, it transpires, is a priority that Benedict inherits from the earlier monastic tradition of the Egyptian desert. To be a good monk is to be able to open your heart to your spiritual elder, it is to expose your 'thoughts' to the elder and to 'dash those thoughts against the rock of Christ' before they grow to unhelpful maturity. 'Thoughts' here is more or less a technical term in monastic literature, referring to chains of fantasy, systems of self-imagining and self-understanding that are primarily self-serving. And because the point of monastic life is to wean us away from self-serving fictions, it becomes crucial to expose those fantasies as something destructive and less than properly human. So monks are exhorted by Benedict 'not to entertain deceit in their heart' (Rule, Chapter 4.24), to acknowledge accountability, to be mindful of death, apart from many other things. 'Not to entertain deceit': not to be enthralled to satisfying fictions about yourself and how you are doing; to accept your share of responsibility in the way things are and the way things go wrong. Honesty is not just about telling the truth to one another, 'in love' or otherwise, it is also about understanding the truth of what *kind* of being you are, which is a mortal being, a fallible being. And part of the offer made by a monastery or church to the public world around is the offer of a certain level of truthfulness about *mortality*. John Maynard Keynes famously said that 'in the long run we are all dead' (1923, p.80); but I think Benedict had something slightly more serious (and positive) in mind than that. The fact that we cannot avoid death means that no one of us has infinite scope or time to realize our aims and our objectives; no one of us has endless time at our disposal, and no one of us is exempt from risk, internal or external.

So these are some of the components of the honesty that is required as a Tool of Good Works. And there is one other interesting phrase that St Benedict uses in this chapter: one of the aspects of the monastic virtue of transparency is 'not to give false peace' (Rule, Chapter 4.25). I think this has something to do with the way in which we can protect ourselves as a community or a society by failing to face conflict, failing to admit the brokenness of our togetherness by making little of it, ignoring it, denying it. It is damaging if we refuse to admit the reality of conflict or to seek a resolution that leaves *me* feeling secure without healing the breach or the offence that others feel. So if we are transparent, honest as part of our growth into communal stability, we have to confront the uncomfortable fact that we are not actually and instinctively at peace with everyone. I certainly do not think that Benedict is recommending a kind of litigious habit of standing by our rights; I do not believe that he is suggesting that we cannot be at peace until justice has been fully done in every way. What he does is to connect the risks of false peace with warnings about anger and resentment, recognizing the fact that anger and resentment can coexist with and reinforce a refusal to name conflict. So being wary of facile reconciliation is not just being suspicious of whether someone else has adequately done justice to *me*. I need fully to acknowledge and deal with my own bewilderment, my own resentment, so that there is a degree of hesitation in me – not about the acceptability of the peace offered by another but about the honesty and depth and integrity of my own desire for peace and willingness to work for it.

Peace

When Benedict speaks of peace in the community's life, then, he is thinking of how the 'circulation' in the body of the community needs to be a circulation of active and imaginative engagement, of clarity about our intentions, rooted in our willingness not to let rivalry and resentment have the last word. Many religious communities will have stories of varying kinds about the visitors who come to them and say 'this is so peaceful'. These stories are told by monks and nuns with a wry smile, because monks and nuns know that within religious communities the last thing you will find, most of the time, is a bland peacefulness. But what presumably communicates to visitors in this sense of a peaceable presence is not that everybody is getting on fine, but that this is a community that works within the parameters of a daily renewed *intention towards* active and honest engagement, a community that assumes there is a stable context within and around relations. It is possible to go beyond rivalry, because the 'currency' exchanged, the flow of life within the community, is about something else, something deeper, about peace.

So in the community, the question is what are we putting into circulation? The great Roman Catholic writer Donald Nicholl, reflecting on his time as head of a college in Jerusalem, touches on this question of 'currency' with his story of an English priest visiting his community who related his experience as a visiting scholar at a university elsewhere. The priest in question was naturally interested in what the 'currency' of the university was, what it was whose circulation helped the working community to stay together, so he spent time trying to uncover what people routinely talked about when they met. At last it dawned on him that the answer to the question of what people were putting into circulation, what people exchanged with one another, was *grievances*. The currency of the university was grievance. For quite a lot of our communities, political, religious and others, putting grievance into circulation, making grudge the fundamental factor that holds them all together, is one of our ways of saving face and protecting ourselves. How then do we put something else into the system? How do we do this without dishonesty, without evasion? We all know in our age that it is bad for us to repress our feelings and that it is poisonous to be passive under injustice. We must acknowledge the risks here, but at the same time, we must recognize that it is so often simpler to put more grudge into the circulation than to break through to something different.

The peace that Benedict was interested in in his monastic community has to be tightly connected with a further point, touched on in this chapter of the 72 Tools, and elaborated elsewhere, a point to do with the level of close attention that is to be given to the specific needs of each member of the community. I will say a word more about this later on, but for now we should note that part of the way he sees authority being exercised in the community has to do with the difficult discernment of what is *most* specific, what is *most* unique about every member. The abbot in the community does not simply issue general instructions but spends the time necessary with each person to see the way that they will function against the background of the stability of the presence of other people: not to encourage them to develop their individuality at everyone's expense, but very particularly how they are to be who they uniquely are *with* these others. That is why abbots lead a very difficult life: a recognition that Benedict does not fudge; that is what they are there for as brokers and agents of the active peacefulness that allows each to be utterly distinct.

Accountability

This, of course, moves us on to the third element, which I have called accountability. The rule of the abbot in Benedict's monastery is not thought of in terms of command. The abbot must first of all be aware that he is responsible for the monks' wellbeing before God. He himself has to be the 'image of Christ' in the monastery, the image of one who takes responsibility for human beings before God. There is a foreshadowing here of Bonhoeffer's extraordinary meditation in his notes on ethics and lectures on Christology, where he speaks of Christ as the one who takes responsibility, who is answerable for human beings as such and requires of his disciples that they share his answerability. Those in authority must, to use Benedict's phrase, 'leaven' the minds of those under their care; they have to allow the doughy, natural texture of the spirit to rise into something more nourishing and bread-like. And Benedict is also, among other things, challenging the ready-made notions of status in his society. The only 'status' that really matters in the monastery is seniority, that is to say, how long you have been in the community, and we could translate this as a way of asking, 'How good are you at stability?' 'Staying the course' is not just a neutral thing for Benedict: those who have been longest in the community know what it is like to live with the others who are not going away, and that is an essential resource for understanding and managing and keeping alive the community around them. But at the same time the abbot has the charge of drawing out of anyone and everyone in the community what they are able to contribute. In a way that is very counter-cultural indeed in the fifth or sixth century; Benedict insists that there are times when the most junior member of the community will actually have something to say that everyone needs to hear. Seniority is not the *only* ground for insight. So the abbot's exercise of authority in this community involves the key discernment both of how to draw on the depth of experience that is there in the senior members and how to avoid that depth of experience just becoming self-confirming and self-perpetuating as the years roll on. The abbot exercises authority with discrimination and distinction, not on the basis of visible differences – whether someone is rich or poor, slave or free in their background – but on the basis of the discernment of their gifts. He is accountable to God; we could also say he is accountable to the distinct and diverse spiritual qualities of those he is dealing with, which is why the Rule can speak not just of obedience to the abbot but of a kind of *mutual* obedience in the community. Novice and senior monk are 'obeying' one another if they are attending with discernment to one another and if the habits that shape their lives are habits of listening, attention and the willingness to take seriously the perspective of the other, the stranger.

The Benedictine monk is someone struggling to live without deceit, his inner life manifest to those to whom he has promised fidelity; he is a person who makes peace by addressing the roots of conflict in himself and the community, a person who attempts to contribute distinctive gifts in such a way as to sustain the circulation of hope and positive expectation in the community, and also the circulation of gifts and insights. But within, behind and through all this, there stands the one great theme of stability: staying with the opportunity community creates to live differently so that we can change and grow as we accompany one another and understand more fully what our humanity is and how it works together.

A rule of life for Parliament Square?

The Benedictine community makes its proposal to the society around in confidence that, while this society may not have chosen to identify with any religious institution, it nonetheless faces all the challenges that Benedict's monks face. As we think about the location of Westminster Abbey in Parliament Square, its triangulation with law and politics, there are a few comparisons that may help us to think this through further. If we are asking about the ethical framework and foundation against which law and politics are set, we would do well to ask some questions about the Benedictine stress on stability. I have already mentioned the way in which we seem always programmed to think that the solution lies in the absence of the other, but Benedict reminds us that our health and wellbeing lie in recognition of the fact that none of us can possess infinite resource or time and so will always need the unexpected stranger to supplement who and what we are. How do we inculcate in law and politics something of that recognition that otherness is not a matter for panic or despair, that the challenge or difficulty of the stranger, the cultural other, the sexual other, the vaguely threatening foreigner at our doors in popular mythology, is potentially a gift? How do we inculcate a political morality that recognizes that these people are not going away and that therefore our task is not to pretend that they can be made to but to work at how we actually engage in transforming our relations with them? That does not of course immediately produce a magical solution, but it flags up the danger of yielding to the temptation of thinking that we can somehow will the stranger into oblivion.

In the same way, to take another major issue, we currently live in a world of almost unimaginable *financial* instability. We have created a seemingly unmanageable engine of chaotic change, governed by a small elite who will determine the patterns of international institutions; a situation in which the vulnerability of national economies to short-term international financial movement is unprecedented. This is one of the most enormous moral challenges before us as a globe, not simply as a society. How do we effectively challenge the currently unchallenged myths about the naturalness or inevitability of this level of financial instability? Is it natural that our societies should be at the mercy of international financial transactions of one kind or another? I have no very neat answers to this; but to shape our questions against the background of the Benedictine question of stability seems a possible way of starting again.

Moving to the three ways in which Benedict thinks through the practical implications of stability, we might explore how we begin discussion with the other sides of Parliament Square about these matters. *Honesty* is not simply the matter of being transparent about your expenses (although that helps). It has something to do with whether or not society expects in its political class a degree of self-criticism and self-questioning or whether it continues (*we* continue) to project unreal expectations, the expectations of problem-solving omnipotence onto its leadership. An honest society ought to be able to guarantee the possibility for those in public life to acknowledge fallibility or uncertainty. It is an ideal that does not seem very close just now. But there is some real urgency about our need to begin inculcating an ethical climate that allows those in public life, those we think of as 'leaders' in our society, to escape from the constraints of our increasingly merciless and unrealistic projections. We also need a far greater clarity about some of the unrealities that are recycled relentlessly in public debate on certain issues: it is astonishing that we are discussing the renewal of Trident in this country – a vastly expensive enterprise in a time of public financial constraint – in a way that seems to allow no mention of the actual risks of nuclear conflict, as if this weaponry's concrete effect were of no interest. Whatever decision might be made about this complex question, it would be reassuring to hear some honest recognition that we are not discussing the choice between a low-risk or risk-free option (retention and improvement of a nuclear weapon) and a reckless bit of idealism but genuinely weighing competing risks. Is it too much to hope that we could have a transparent debate on this?

Peacefulness is a rather obvious extension to this discussion. It does not, as I said earlier, mean a bland denial or evasion of conflict. What it does mean is a resolution to address conflict without despair, in the confidence that not everything must be dictated by rivalry and violence. So the question here is how we inculcate a political culture of willingness to go on arguing civilly, staging and negotiating real difference without premature panic or resorting to the familiar urge to cancel the other. Civil disagreement is part of the health of a working society, a natural next step when we have been talking about honesty in debate. And if we are afraid of, nervous about, honesty because we are afraid of some kind of exposure of weakness, we need to be reminded of the strength that comes from solidarity and mutual trust as opposed to the constant struggle of isolation. Perhaps we can yet learn how to conduct arguments well, how to live as what I have sometimes called in the past an argumentative democracy – that is, not simply a formal democracy with voting and representative protocols, but one where civil society is articulate and brave enough to have arguments about fundamental issues in public without fear of this descending into recrimination, abuse and ultimately violence. As is often observed, this is more to do with culture than law, but the institutions around us in this Square will not work as they should unless this corner of the Square is doing what it can to shape a culture of positive disagreement, of argumentative civil speech. In particular, for the church and the monastic community to model an active plurality of gift and vision working together is clearly a focal aspect of the gift and offer made to society and its institutions.

And the *accountability* of society's institutions has to do, quite simply, with the question of how far a political class (and of course its equivalent in the church) is visibly and publicly answerable to the good of those they lead. That is the fundamental question: not whether such and such a political group or agency is the purveyor of a persuasive or even an effective policy in terms that make sense to me and people like me, but whether that group is thinking clearly and honestly about its accountability for the wellbeing of the entire society it serves. To use a shorthand familiar from Catholic Social Teaching, it is an accountability to the common good. If government, parties, activist groups and devolved authorities are willing to discuss and demonstrate that sort of accountability, then I would say that functionally, for all practical purposes, they are demonstrating their accountability to *God* – to the extent that they are putting aside private and partial agendas for the honour and wellbeing of all made in the divine image.

So the questions to our political culture, our questions about legislation and styles of government and so on, need to be connected to the question of how political leadership might embody in its own way, its own style, what Benedict in the Rule defines as stable and nurturing habits. It will entail asking whether our models of leadership can exhibit, for example: a deeply ingrained suspicion of any ready-made solutions that arise from uncritical veneration for a given social status; a deep commitment to examining the particularities of the needs of persons or groups and a reluctance to work with generalities, let alone clichés; a willingness to listen to those on the margin, as well as those who appear to have inbuilt authority. Those three elements that I have picked up from

Benedict's Rule – honesty, peacefulness and accountability – thus converge in a potential new configuring of political ethics. The 'offer' that the Benedictine tradition makes, and ultimately the offer that the Christian tradition itself makes, is of a kind of life that works differently from the patterns we assume to be obvious. It involves an attempt to model ways of living together, ways of exercising authority and ways of conducting a public debate or dispute against the background of a basic recognition that we have no choice but to take time with one another, with the other who is not going away, and so to use positively the background of relations that do not depend on our choice or taste so as to learn new ways of deciding and new ways of honouring each other. In this context, we have to go on asking the sort of difficult questions I sketched earlier about how public policy creates or fails to create stability, how it does or does not point us to ways in which our social environment could be regarded as trustworthy. One of the very worst things that can happen to society is for it to arrive at a point where a critical mass of the population no longer has confidence that the social environment is dependable and so concludes that they have no stake in the matter. Just how close are we to this in Britain today?

Concluding thoughts

As I said earlier on, the Benedictine monastery and the Church of God overall are intentional communities; not everybody joins them. We have no way of saying to the world around, 'You *have* to believe all this and act accordingly'; as a bare matter of fact, we cannot make that happen. But what we can say is that here are the signs by which we measure social and communal health – and its absence. That is the heart of what the Christian community, Benedictine or otherwise, says in the political sphere – in Parliament Square. But ultimately, for the believing community, all of this depends on something much deeper and more fundamental: the stability that we see in God. For Benedict and for all Christian communities, their life is possible because of the underlying belief that God is to be trusted. God is stable, and it is against the background of that stability that our own probing and uncertainty, our own unevenly successful attempts to embody all this, generally make whatever sense they manage to. They have a meaning and a depth, a reference to that without which nothing else happens. Benedict's Rule is framed by his assumption that all of us struggling to master the Tools of Good Works are finally oriented towards something much more radical in terms of contemplative self-offering, in terms of solitude and intensity of communion; the Rule ends by referring us onwards to the example of the Desert Fathers. Only when we have discovered something about honesty, peace and accountability can we even think, in Benedict's world, of moving on to 'higher' levels of spiritual life. He is, you might say, reminding us that it is very problematic to try to be too spiritual too soon, to assume that you can find a spiritual life independently of these very prosaic values of transparency, peace-making and responsibility, fleshed out in the 'political' life of the community, even the small community of the monastery.

So when the church makes its offer, and when Benedict makes his proposal to the political and legal world around, it is a proposal for laying the foundations of something that could lead to a great deal more than just the 'prose' of community, but the prose still has to be written. The patience, the doggedness of endurance, the commitment to let yourself be challenged to be more honest – all this points to a depth of stability that ultimately allows prose to be transformed into something else, in imagination, art, contemplation, the mystical, the creative, indeed, in science as much as art. Shape your basic humanity aright, and that humanity will become something extraordinary; pinch and reduce the prosaic habits of your daily humanity, and do not be too surprised if the world shrinks. It is true that to a superficial observer 'society at large' does not seem to have very much to do with the Benedictine enterprise as the Holy Rule describes it. Benedict assumes that the primary work of his monks is to worship and keep silence, acknowledging the roots of their calling and the possibilities it carries. Yet society, as we have seen, with or without those moments of recollection and rooting, has to manage those things that keep humanity moving and growing. It needs resources to handle these things well rather than evasively or superficially, and the Rule of Benedict gives fundamental advice for how we grow as human beings.

The Tools of Good Works in the Holy Rule are simply tools for becoming human as we are meant to be. And the Rule's basic ethic of candour, respect and patience is what Benedict assumes we have to master before we can do anything else. That is why the resulting insights I have suggested are by no means irrelevant to Westminster Abbey's neighbour institutions. And as we think about the role of those neighbour institutions, we are of course going to come back to the deeply uncomfortable matter of how far we exhibit any loyalty to Benedict's ethic within our diverse religious institutions, how far the transparent and trustworthy harmony of Benedict's community is allowed to be visible among us. But that no doubt is a matter for another occasion.

Benedictine Values in Public Life

Three Essays by Vernon White,
Andrew Tremlett
and Claire Foster-Gilbert

Introduction

We are living through turbulent times. Westminster Abbey
has seen many of these over its thousand-year history, and
it has a responsibility to the public service institutions by
which it is surrounded to provide the stability that comes from
historical perspective, work hard to be a reminder of lasting
incommensurable values over and above economic ones and
steadfastly keep retuning to goodness, however fallibly, when
there are such polarized views of what goodness might be, in
the political sphere and in the country as a whole.

When Westminster Abbey needs to regenerate its own
moral heart, it digs down into its Benedictine roots. Benedict
of Nursia (480–547) on whose Rule Rowan Williams drew
in his previous essay, is responsible for a way of monastic

life that inspired communities the world over, but especially in Europe, of which he is a patron saint. Westminster Abbey is a Benedictine Foundation, and although it lost its monastic habit in the Elizabethan Settlement following the Reformation, it does not forget its original inspiration.

Benedict is also the patron saint of speleologists, cave explorers. The following three essays explore Benedictine values: stability, community and the conversion of manners or morals, and can be read in the spirit of returning to the back of one's cave, as it were, for restoration and renewal.

Anyone who has sincerely tried to live a good life, whether it be through eating a healthy diet, taking regular exercise, studying, meditating or praying, will know that it is nearly impossible to succeed when there are others about, who make demands, have different priorities and always complicate things. But we also know that it is nearly impossible to be true to a good life *without* the support of others. Benedict's Rule addresses this conundrum, and as nations around the world readjust to their senses of themselves both in themselves and in relation to others, at a time when global collaboration – not competition – was never more needed, so Benedict's scholarship and spirituality is all the more worth drawing upon: an intelligent offer from an ancient and lively past.

Claire Foster-Gilbert

STABILITY

Recovering the Lost Icon
of Creative Fidelity

Vernon White

The thesis of this essay is, in essence, very simple. It is this: our personal and social life needs a measure of stability; our current social context is intrinsically *de*-stabilizing in some key respects; and in this context the stability we need to recover is not primarily a new political programme or legal framework but a particular disposition of character or cast of mind: namely, the disposition of creative faithfulness.

Faithfulness is now a largely unfashionable disposition. But I believe it is a vital condition, or frame of reference, for any stable personal or social order. As such it is what Rowan Williams (2000) would describe as a social and cultural 'icon'. (Williams himself does not cite faithfulness as one of our key social icons; the point of this essay is to make the case for it.) This proposal that faithfulness is a key component of stability is hardly a new insight: it is ancient, grounded deep in the origins of western philosophy and in the heart of Christian theology, about which I will say more later. But it is an insight that I think is particularly critical now, not least because it has currently lost that iconic status.

What follows, then, is first an explanation of why it is particularly important now, an exposition of what I actually mean by 'faithfulness', some illustrations of its role in specific areas of personal life and social order and finally, as a reassurance that this is not just a personal or idiosyncratic take on life, a brief recapitulation of its deep roots in wider western philosophy and Christian thought.

Social fluidity, identity and change: a critical context for faithfulness

First, why so critical now? This is chiefly because of the context we now inhabit in late-modern social life and the intensity and peculiar nature of change to which it subjects us. The rapid, interconnected changes caused by information technology, cultural globalization and the economic drive to stimulate constant new consumer demand do not just affect us trivially but also affect our very identity, our sense of who we are. And this is intrinsically destabilizing.

It starts early. Children and teenagers are not just passively receiving the changing images of terrestrial television, they also interact actively online with a multitude of other changing anonymous virtual bloggers, tweeters and game players, from anywhere in the world, from whom they constantly absorb lifestyles, political views, values and prejudices that relativize everything previously inherited, offering instead a multitude of new identities. This condition of 'liquid modernity', as sociologist Zygmunt Bauman (2000) has described it, typifies adult life too. We are all exposed through various media to a torrent of options. These options are not superficial. They do not just concern different goods to buy but also deeper lifestyle priorities, beliefs and values. These inevitably unsettle our family structures, allegiance to institutions, religions, moralities – and so, again, this affects our very identity, our sense of who we are. We are also destabilized by the changes it brings in others around us, in family, friends and colleagues. When, for example, I find I can no longer relate to my neighbour as husband of his first wife, teacher and New Labour supporter, but must now relate to him as partner of his new boyfriend, software consultant and politically detached, who I am in relation to him also changes. Multiply this with others changing around me, and I am destabilized even more. And we should not underestimate how disturbing this can be. To be constantly unsure who we are or who others are, to be always on the cusp of the unknown with others and ourselves, evokes a sense of loss, fear, disintegration and mortality. It is a cause of high rates of stress in individuals and a cause of strain in society generally. Without any settled identities, our family life, civic life and institutional life, which depend on relatively settled values, continuities and commitments, all tend to disintegrate. That is why 'change and *decay*', as a famous hymn puts it, often seem to go together.

This is not for one moment to suggest that all change is destructive, and decay is all that we see. Emphatically not. Change and reinvention of ourselves and others is in fact often highly positive in both personal life and social order. A fixed, frozen, *un*changing persona in individuals is often a sign of spiritual death, whereas change in ourselves is often a sign of spiritual life, creativity and liberation. In social terms too, change is of course often very progressive, freeing us from false identities imposed by oppressive social systems. Social change has freed women from fixed roles determined by men and freed gay people from discrimination. Change in education, refusing to pigeon-hole children with fixed identities at, say, the age of 11, has allowed them to flourish with late development and life-long learning. All this sort of fluidity and change is clearly positive. And in any case, seeing all change as threat simply fails the test of history. Rapid change happened in the past and we did not disintegrate then. As critic Frank Kermode has pointed out, much of our current fluid social condition is just a mirror of social revolutions of the nineteenth century that actually brought benefits.

Even so, while fully accepting this, there is a distinctive twist to the nature of change we now experience that is particularly destabilizing. This lies in the fact that much current change is without any clear direction; we do not have a clear sense of where we are heading with it. This is a function of the wider situation we inhabit, commonly called post-modernity, in which we have largely lost confidence in any agreed overall stories to help us deal with or interpret change. Overall stories of life offered by science, politics, cultural theory and religion are still available, but none now commands any real consensus; they are fragmented by pluralism. So when a new idea or experience occurs there is no agreed coherent story by which we can evaluate its meaning. Instead, we are simply left to create a meaning for ourselves. And the trouble is, these purely self-chosen meanings are bound to be more fragile, transient and isolating.

So for example, listening to 16- to 18-year-olds, I have seen this in the way they often handle new ideas. In a recent discussion about genetic engineering of children they did not assess the issue against any overall world-view, whether that of religious belief about God's unique image in humanity or of scientific belief about the evolution of humanity. Instead, they interpreted it in much the same way they respond to a new piece of popular music. That is, the moral question was effectively reduced to an individual aesthetic judgement: do I *like* the idea; does it suit my tastes? Briefly this may feel like liberation from having moral views just imposed by tradition. But in the longer term it is isolating and stressful. When major moral and existential issues are *just* down to me to choose, I can become overwhelmed.

Leaving things just to our own preference makes us vulnerable not only to stress but also to fundamentalism: that is, it invites totalitarian certainty to replace the confusions of choice. In fact, we become vulnerable to any kind of dogmatic influence or institution that exploits the confusion for its own purposes, whether religious, political or financial. In other words, any social context that by design or default, appears to leave us to personal preference in our morality and identity may not really make us free: it may simply make us more easy prey to others.

All this is an effect of current forms of change and instability crying out for a reordered disposition with which to address it. That is, it requires a new default social habit that can give some stability in our identity through the experience of change, yet without denying change; a disposition sufficiently grounded in a collective world-view to give it more staying power than purely personal preference, yet also sufficiently flexible to survive in a plural world. And this, I believe, is exactly what we find in faithfulness.

Commitment and creativity: meanings of faithfulness

But what do I really mean by 'faithfulness'? Social philosopher Alasdair MacIntyre (1981) has provided one of the best clues to this. His book *After Virtue* offers a brilliant and prescient analysis of social instability, which ends with a call for a new Benedict to save us. *Prima facie* this is surprising. A cryptic appeal to a sixth-century Christian monk may seem to sit oddly in a largely secular analysis. But it is entirely apposite. For Benedict in his own unstable times had in fact identified the very form of faithfulness that I believe we need now. He displayed it specifically as a rule for a monastic community, but it can be readily extended to a wider remit.

Specifically, it is what I shall call 'creative fidelity'. Creative fidelity has two key elements. First it is a serious, sustained and (if necessary) sacrificial commitment to the wellbeing of a person or institution through both time and space: that is, a commitment to someone or something through a long narrative of past, present and future, not just in the present moment; it is also a commitment exercised in a narrative that includes the subject's relations with others, not just the subject considered in isolation according to his or her own current sense of wellbeing. This sort of 'holistic' fidelity is what uniquely gives identity and stability to unstable people and institutions through time and change. It also gives identity to the one being faithful. It is a commitment, as philosopher Josiah Royce (1908, p.863) said, which 'unifies a life, gives it centre, fixity, stability'. Faithfulness in this sense becomes a virtuous circle replacing the vicious circle of destabilization for all concerned. Without this sort of faithfulness, as Milan Kundera describes in *The Unbearable Lightness of Being* (2000), we all splinter into fragments; with it we can all recover solidity, integrity and stability.

The vital second element, however, is this: such faithfulness does not just mean a commitment to be doggedly there for someone, some cause or some institution in the long term, it also means being *creatively* there for them; that is, it means being willing to look for new ways to relate constructively to that wider narrative of the other's life. In other words, it is not something that simply locks us into unchanging attitudes, absolute rules, unyielding dogmas; it is certainly not blind loyalty. It is much more dynamic, even critical if necessary, in its constancy. French Catholic philosopher Gabriel Marcel (1949), who coined the phrase creative fidelity, describes it as no passive 'inertia' of the soul but as a creative changing response to the presence of another person (or institution) who themselves are alive and changing. So, as such, it positively embraces and harnesses change to deal with change. It is a disposition that incorporates the positive role of change even in its attempt to re-establish stability. That, in brief, is what I mean by creative fidelity.

Family life and working practices: creative fidelity in personal and social praxis

All this could be demonstrated in almost any area of social and personal life. I will explore just two: that is, two fields of human experience where change is rife, where our sense of identity is deeply implicated and where the icon of creative fidelity is particularly ripe for reinstatement. The first is the way we order and understand our close personal relationships; the second is the way we order our working relationships and practices. Neither is exclusive to public servants, of course, but both are highly pertinent to them.

First, close personal relationships of friendship, sexual partnerships, marriage and family life. These are clearly constitutive of who we are and how we operate, and they have certainly changed. In fact, they have always changed. Social patterns of kinship have always been shifting. But not always at the present rate and in this directionless way that we have now experienced over past decades. So sociologist Anthony Giddens (1991), for example, has suggested that there is at least one overall fundamental change now in all our personal relationships, even family relationships. This is a shift towards a more 'reflexive', self-referential project. That is, we now tend to choose, assess and fashion our relationships more in terms of their direct impact on our own personal experience, rather than as part of a wider public or social role or duty; and as such we are more likely to end relationships when they do not quickly deliver that personal experience we want.

What effect does this have? The publicly measurable consequences are clear: an increase in the divorce rate, single-parent families, absent fathers and non-marital births; a profusion of different forms of temporary co-habitation; a decrease in all long-term relationships. Consequences for the private texture of our experience of relationships are harder to measure. But Giddens has tried. His observation is that this change has generated relationships of more intensity, excitement and instant emotional honesty. But at the same time, relationships are tending to be more unstable and inward-looking and less engaged with wider public life and public roles.

This change is not all bad. Far from it. A desire for inward intensity has unlocked new honesty and satisfaction compared with the formalized, emotionally frozen nature of some past forms of fixed relationship. Fluidity in personal relationships has given new possibilities for gay and transgender people. As I said before, it has meant liberation for women previously locked into oppressive relationships. And much literature in the 1960s and 70s has stressed these benefits.

But, of course, what we also see, documented more in literature from the 1980s onwards, is destabilizing effects as well: personal stress and social damage. The quest for short-term, self-referring emotional intensity and satisfaction has meant we cut and run too quickly to find a new relationship when the satisfaction fades, rather than staying to discover new satisfactions *within* an existing one. This then brings those obvious consequences of transient relationships: if there are children they can be damaged by the insecurity this brings; if there are elderly dependants they can be neglected if they seem unable to provide that sort of reciprocal intensity of relationship. In fact, anyone of any age or gender can be damaged simply because of this pressure of a high emotional expectation and the threat of transience in a relationship. To feel under constant pressure to form new relationships and roles to meet these expectations inevitably causes stress and breakdown. This in turn then feeds yet more instability into our relationships. It is a vicious circle. To be sure, this is not a picture of all actual relationships. But it is a real and observable trend.

Clearly, then, this is an obvious and critical domain for creative fidelity. It requires exactly a disposition whose instinctive goal is not just short-term, transient satisfaction for ourselves but the much more interesting and satisfying project of sharing the long-term narrative of someone else's life, and to do so creatively, not just doggedly. And the point is, this is a particularly credible and realistic disposition to propose in this context. For although its overall orientation to long-term commitment may be counter-cultural, it is not simply proposing fixed, absolute, rules about relationships; it is still a creative, dynamic disposition, and in that sense it fits with a fluid culture, as well as challenging it.

Hard cases will demonstrate this credibility. For example, can creative faithfulness even make sense in situations of an irretrievable breakdown of relationships? Or can it make sense when relating to someone in the last stages of dementia when personality has wholly changed? I think it can. The key is precisely in the way this disposition holds us to seeing the whole narrative of someone's life, not just the most recent episode (whether dementia or divorce). In the case of severe dementia, creative fidelity helps maintain some form of relationship precisely by holding us to try to see the person not only as they are with us now, but also as they once were (and, with Christian faith, how they will be too, in eternity). In the case of losing a partner by irretrievable breakdown, it is not dissimilar. To be able to see the former partner as they were, not just as they are, and in the wider narrative of their other relationships into the future as well (that is, to be able to see him or her not only as the one leaving us but also as the continuing father or mother of the children, the continuing friend of our friends) can be creative and constructive. It can help to honour the relationship positively in some new form, even when its previous form has ended.

This is not fantasy. Research cited by Giddens (Stacey 1990) in Silicon Valley in the US, where there has long been widespread family breakdown, suggests that this is actually happening to such an extent that it is now embedded in new social patterns. People there have already created new forms of loyalty to former partners by formalizing patterns of communication between step-families in new social conventions of expected social interaction; a way of continuing to honour previous relationships, thereby creating new forms of social stability. In 1990 a Church of England report on 'ageing' was sceptical, claiming that we do not yet know what loyalty there may be to step-parents. But clearly there *can* be such loyalties; that is, loyalties in the wider family relationships set up between new and former partners. What is key in making this more possible is precisely when the disposition of creative fidelity becomes a social norm and gets embedded and reinforced in wider culture and convention, not just individual choice.

The second domain of social life I wish to cite is the culture of working relationships and the practices that govern them. This too can be fundamental to our sense of identity. It is also certainly a site of change and of strain. Rational managerial theory and economic drivers have seen to that. It is an area where creative fidelity ought to be relevant. So can we extend this disposition, realistically, into that area as well? Could we see this disposition worked out in actual praxis here too?

The particular context of change here, very broadly speaking, is a shift from settled occupations, whether mining, ship-building or plumbing, or settled careers in a city bank or commercial company, to portfolio work, short-term consultancy and project-based work. And the consequences in many ways mirror what has been going on in our personal relationships. On the one hand, it has freed up labour, bringing economic benefit to companies and personal benefits of intense short-term satisfaction when individual projects come to fruition. But on the other hand, this fluidity has also often produced a hollowed-out work culture bereft of long-term personal loyalties and trust, undermining the worth, satisfaction and identity of belonging long-term to companies and institutions. This means that even where the rhetoric of loyalty and belonging to a team is often employed, this is largely spurious, as business analysts readily concede, because the culture actually depends on many short-term relationships.

Again, the 1990s brought especially acute awareness of this. A survey of managerial careers in 1995, for example, concluded that project-based work and fluidity of employment has led to 'an environment [which] has caused the loss of the long-term relational contract...[which] implied mutual commitment and trust over the long-term' (Herriot and Pemberton 1995, p.xv). A more recent Demos report (Flores and Gray 2000, p.23) shows the trend continuing; it suggests, 'experiencing the passion involved in achieving a particular personal goal now largely replaces loyalty to institutions and communities'. This certainly produces strain. There is the obvious strain of insecurity. But there is also an even deeper rupture in our identity, for if this work culture means I must operate with radically different values at work and home – that is, working for short-term personal success in the former, but long-term sharing of life in the latter – then I am literally dis-integrated.

Again, this is not a picture of all actual work experience. But it is an observable trajectory. So this too is surely a key area to relearn creative fidelity (or in this context, perhaps creative 'loyalty' is the better language). What is needed is a default disposition of loyalty, in both employer and employee, which leads them to want to recover satisfactions of long-term mutual achievement. To be clear: this is not loyalty understood as a disposition that stifles the economic and personal advantages of change; it is loyalty as a bedrock *for* change. It is not loyalty as a fossilizing inertia, but as a basis for the sort of stable personal relationships at work that generate more energy, purpose, creativity and confidence to critique the *status quo*. This is in contrast to short-term, purely target-driven, contractual relationships, which can dissipate energy, creativity and confidence simply through the stress of insecurity.

In this domain too, it is not fantasy to think it might be possible. Some companies and institutions do now attempt to honour the wider narrative of their workers' and members' lives. It is done, for example, by offering longer term career progression with training so that an individual's identity and gifts are not atomized at work, exploited just for the present and then cast aside, but rather offered continuity and harnessed to other areas of work. Some employers also now honour the wider narrative of a worker's life beyond work altogether. This is done, for example, by encouraging social engagement, volunteering and wider public duty so that work values and personal values of the employee are more integrated. In other words, these are already genuine 'new deals' at work, as described by a recent report on managerial careers, offering practical and realistic structures for creative loyalty.

From social commitment to Christian revelation

One reason why this disposition is realistic, whether at work or in any other context, is simply because it is wanted as well as needed. 'Commitment' is not a dirty word, for young or old. In spite of all counter-pressures of late-modern consumer society, and in spite of all short-term, purely self-satisfying instincts of human nature (evolutionary or just plain sinful), we do retain a longing for wider, deeper commitments in life.

And it is this that now brings me to a final point. If we reflect on this deeper longing for commitment that feeds the disposition of creative fidelity, it cries out for further explanation, as surely as those other features of human experience described in previous essays about idealism. It begs the question: what exactly is this longing? What is its authority? Where does its resilience come from in the face of such powerful cultural oppositions? What is its ultimate source?

One source is Benedict. As indicated before, he was undoubtedly appealing to stability for his community, right back in the sixth century in the instabilities of his time. In his celebrated Rule he was scathing about what he called the worst kind of monks 'always on the move...mere slaves to their own wills and appetites' (Rule, Chapter 1), *but* he was also flexible in his rule for them. He was, therefore, an early source of something very like creative fidelity.

It surely goes back further too. There was a crucible for creative fidelity even back in pre-Socratic Greek philosophy, in the debate between Heraclitus and Parmenides and the sort of world that, between them, they perceived. Heraclitus saw the fundamental stuff of reality, the real womb of all life, in flux, difference and change, whereas Parmenides (and later Plato) saw it in oneness, stability and consistency, as the ultimate ground of all this change. So perhaps it is in that symbiotic tension between flux and constancy that creative fidelity was born – as the only practical disposition that will actually work in this sort of complex world.

Then there is its origin in Christian revelation itself, to which, of course, Benedict was most indebted. It actually lies at the very heart of Christian faith in its most fundamental grasp of the nature of God Himself/Herself. It arose when theologians saw the tension between flux and constancy to be in God's own self and refused the polarity; that is, when they insisted on God as Trinity, as an eternal interplay of three persons, yet in one relationship, thereby combining *both* flux and stability as ultimates in His/Her own being.

This doctrinal reality is also concretely expressed in the narratives of scripture. There God constantly projects His identity in the history of Israel, and in the person of Christ, precisely as a God of creative fidelity who combines flux and stability. The narratives consistently show who God is ('I am who I am'/'I will be who I will be') in the way God keeps long-term covenant faith with people, that is, love shown *through time*, which is what faithfulness is. God shows Himself as one who kept faith with them even in wilderness and exile with a fidelity, a consistent character, wholly unlike the other capricious gods around. This God is then shown decisively in Christ as one who kept faith even at the cost of the cross, undeterred by betrayal, desertion and death. It is a specifically creative fidelity throughout, because in this long narrative God shows fidelity by doing new things, not simply by demonstrating an unchanging eternal essence.

In short, the seeds of this disposition really do lie deep. They lie right back in ancient Greek and Hebrew world-views and above all in the Christian synthesis of both – our deepest sources of western moral and social tradition. And that is what lends it such authority and resonance.

One final question provoked by this: if it has such pedigree, why, we may ask, has it nonetheless faded? Why has it become a largely lost icon? The obvious answer is that it has been just another inevitable casualty of liberal modernity. And that is borne out in intellectual history. When I looked into the history of loyalty and faithfulness in intellectual tradition I found that few since the Enlightenment had given it any serious and extended consideration (except for that early twentieth-century idealist philosopher Josiah Royce, hardly a household name!).

This could mean its future is considered bleak. If liberalism is the cause of its demise it may seem unlikely it will ever be retrieved, in spite of those deep roots and its resonance with some of our deepest longings. But I do not think so, and not just because liberalism is itself now changing and we enter what many consider to be a post-liberal time. For I suspect that any demise of fidelity has anyway been much more to do with a misunderstanding than a necessary consequence of liberalism. The misunderstanding is that a call to faithfulness is always and only a reactionary call, a failure of nerve in breaking out of the *status quo*, just blind loyalty, which would indeed be anathema to liberalism. What I hope to have made clear is how wrong that is. Creative fidelity, as Benedict knew, is actually a progressive, life-giving, healing, dynamic disposition, not reactionary at all.

So perhaps we can and will relearn it after all, even now in today's more fluid climate. I certainly hope so.

COMMUNITY
Andrew Tremlett

Introduction

The often-repeated words of John Donne's Meditation xvii from his *Devotions upon Emergent Occasions* give a starting point for this essay's consideration of 'community':

> No man is an island entire of itself;

Usually, the quotation from Donne is restricted to this single line, though on occasion it is expanded to include the more sombre:

> any man's death diminishes me,
> because I am involved in mankind.
> And therefore never send to know for whom
> the bell tolls; it tolls for thee.

But given the fundamental change initiated by the United Kingdom electorate during the European Union Referendum of June 2016, Donne's writing seems to be extraordinarily prescient!

> No man is an island entire of itself; every man
> is a piece of the continent, a part of the main;

if a clod be washed away by the sea, *Europe*
is the less, as well as if a promontory were, as
well as any manner of thy friends or of thine
own were; any man's death diminishes me,
because I am involved in mankind.
And therefore never send to know for whom
the bell tolls; it tolls for thee.

All this is by way of introducing this second essay on 'Benedictine values in public life', drawing on the tradition that has so shaped not only Westminster Abbey, but also more widely the institutions that sit around Parliament Square. Taken between the two chapters on the more recognizably Benedictine values of stability and the conversion of manners, this consideration of community focuses on how the monastic tradition has framed the conversation around the creation of what we might call closely interdependent living, particularly in terms of assimilation or socialization upon entry.

While 'community' is now a political catchphrase that covers everything from Big Society to BAME (Black, Asian, Minority Ethnic), Westminster has its origins in a distinct and defined monastic community that has left its imprint on both church and state. Where did this sense of community come from and to what extent is it still important today? How do the institutions and instruments of government mediate between society at large and communities in particular? Or perhaps, as Donne would put it, what is the impact of the human reality that 'No man is an island entire of itself' when considering the institutions of state?

Admission to the community in
the Benedictine tradition

Benedict of Nursia, the founding father of the western monastic tradition that bears his name, wrote his Rule towards the end of his life (he died in 547) having established the monastery at Monte Cassino, the place where he put pen to paper. Its 73 chapters lay out a vast range of areas governing community life, and it was the reading of a chapter from this Rule that gave both the name and meaning to the Chapter House, which was a standard feature of every major monastery, including at pre-Reformation Westminster Abbey.

But among the most important, Chapter 58 is about how the monastic community is to be formed and replenished, 'Of the Manner of Admitting Brethren', p.89. In human resources terms, this is the recruitment process. And, to be brutally frank, it is not altogether encouraging. One might have expected that a religious community would be only too happy to see new members join their ranks and refill the reservoirs with fresh, keen and energetic novices. Nothing could be further from the truth:

> Newcomers to the monastic life should not be granted easy entry, but as the Apostle says, 'Test the spirits to see whether they are from God' (1 John 4:1). If the newcomer persists in knocking and seems to endure patiently the harsh treatment and the difficulty of entry, and if he continues to make his petition, then he should be allowed in and permitted to stay for a few days in the guest-house.

So we are describing here a process of discernment, rather than an open-door policy. And, for the avoidance of doubt, participation in the community is not about joining in or even wanting to pray with others, it is about a change of life, the *conversatio morum* or the 'conversion of manners', which is the subject of the next essay in this series.

And then begins a year-long process of testing the postulant, the one who is seeking to be admitted, trying their vocation, 'The novice should be told about all the difficult and harsh things he will experience along the road to God (p.91).'

At regular intervals of two months – six months – four months, the Rule of St Benedict is read to him or her in its entirety so that this would-be novice understands absolutely and fully, to the best of their knowledge and as far as they know themselves, what they are undertaking. This is testing by any standards:

> If, after careful consideration, he promises to observe all the rules and to obey all the commands given to him, then he should be received into the community, in full awareness of the fact that the law of the rule lays down that from that day on he is not allowed to leave the monastery or to withdraw his neck from the yoke of the rule, which he had been allowed to accept or reject during the extended period of reflection. (p.91)

In almost literal terms, you made your bed; now you must lie in it! But what comes next is the taking of vows, which, rather like a marriage, is performed before God and in front of the gathered congregation of the community:

> The one who is to be received should take a vow in the oratory in front of everyone: he must promise stability, conversion of his way of life and obedience before God and his saints, so that if he ever does otherwise, he will be clear that he will be condemned by the one whom he scorns. (p.90)

Clearly, this is not a personal undertaking or a private vow. It is not quite sealed in blood, but the new member writes – if he is able to do so – an account of his promise, and the gathered community repeats three times a verse from Psalm 119, 'Uphold me, O Lord, according to Thy word and I shall live; and let me not be confounded in my expectations.'

The ritual process of entering the community is completed by a physical stripping away of any resources that the novice brings into the community, casting himself down before his brothers, and then his being re-vested in the garb of the monastery, similar to the vesting of the newly baptized. Intriguingly, his old clothes are to be retained in case – God forbid – the Devil should ever persuade him to leave the community.

What is evident from this gradual process of introduction, integration and indoctrination, is that the vows of stability, the conversion of morals and obedience are symbolic of the community the novice is entering. The taking of vows has a sacramental quality, an outward symbol of an inward grace. But it is the community being entered that provides the context and actualization for those vows – without community, vows are merely good and noble intentions, unrealized aspirations.

So the initial point of this essay is that *community* does not happen by itself. If nothing else, Chapter 58 of the Rule of St Benedict tells us that creating *community* is intentional, hard work and sacrificial. It involves a fixed purpose, a clear commitment and a willingness to set aside personal wants and ambitions for the sake of the greater good. If the high ideals and aspirations of the vows taken are the seed, community is the soil in which those hopes flourish and thrive or wither and die.

Understanding community

One of the most striking features of this subject area is how fluidly the word 'community' is used. Etymologically it is derived from the Old French *communeté*, which in turn comes from the Latin *communitas* (itself from *communis*: 'things held in common'). But a quick scan of recent headlines reveals a wide range of contemporary contexts. A few examples will give a flavour: 'Pillars of the community'; 'Community continues to embrace social diversity'; 'Community or district nursing'; 'survivors' rights advocates in the community have long complained of a cover-up culture'; 'A much-loved community orchard'. In Westminster there is a Department for Communities and Local Government, whose 2016 objectives include 'to create great places to live and work, and to give more power to local people to shape what happens in their area'.

So 'community' is being used in a wide range of contexts to cover a whole spectrum of meanings. But are there more fundamental understandings of community, frameworks which might help us interpret how society at large interacts with particular localities? And, more importantly, in an era when people appear to relate more readily through social media or associational means rather than geographical connections, how might these theoretical frameworks help us to 'read' more accurately what is going on in the very particular community gathered around Parliament Square?

Early research in the nineteenth century by the German sociologist, Ferdinand, described two types of human association set out in his work *Gemeinschaft und Gesellschaft* (Tönnies 1957, first published 1887), roughly translated as 'community' and 'society/association'. *Gemeinschaft* stresses personal social interactions and the roles, values and beliefs based on them; *Gesellschaft*, on the other hand, looks more towards indirect interactions, impersonal roles, formal roles and beliefs. *Gemeinschaft* refers to groupings based on feelings of togetherness and on mutual bonds, which are felt as a goal to be kept up, their members being the means for this goal. *Gesellschaft* refers to groups that are sustained by it being instrumental for their members' individual aims and goals. The equilibrium in *Gemeinschaft* is achieved through morals, conformism and exclusion – social control – while *Gesellschaft* keeps its equilibrium through police, laws, tribunals and prisons.

Gerhard Delanty (2003) in his work *Community* talks about the increasing individualism of modern western society being accompanied by an enduring nostalgia for the idea of community as a source of security and belonging and, in recent years, as an alternative to the state as a basis for politics. He sets out three understandings of community:

- *Location-based communities* or communities of place.

- *Identity-based communities*, which range from religious, faith-based communities, to multicultural and pluralistic societies.

- *Organizationally based communities* from communities clustered informally around family to more formal incorporated associations.

More recently, Paul James (2012) in his work on sustainable communities, has proposed a nuanced and perhaps more useful understanding:

- *Grounded community relations*: This involves enduring attachment to particular places and particular people. It is the dominant form taken by customary and tribal communities. In these kinds of communities, the land is fundamental to identity.

- *Lifestyle community relations*: This involves giving primacy to communities coming together around particular chosen ways of life, such as morally charged or interest-based relations, or just living or working in the same location. Some examples might be: i) community life as morally bounded, a form taken by many traditional faith-based communities; ii) community life as interest-based, including sporting, leisure-based and business communities that come together for regular moments of engagement; iii) community life as proximately related, where neighbourhood or commonality of association forms a community of convenience or a community of place.

- *Projected community relations*: This is where a community is self-consciously treated as an entity to be projected and recreated. It can be projected through an advertising slogan, for example for a gated as an entity or can take the form of ongoing associations of people who seek political integration; communities of practice based on professional projects; associative communities that seek to enhance and support individual creativity, autonomy and mutuality. A nation is, in a sense, one of the largest forms of projected or imagined community.

These are only models, of course, imagined and idealized super-structures that we overlay on experience to make sense of what we see and perceive in the world around us. Grounded community relations, for example, are not restricted to tribal communities in remote regions. Coming from Devon, I have a very strong sense of the land, of what Aboriginal peoples in Australia call 'Country': a deep sense of connectedness with the soil itself. Lifestyle community relations are easy to spot in the Park Run experience, where thousands of people gather on a Sunday morning to do their five-kilometre run in parks up and down the country. They are also evident in the choices made to live in a religious community, whether in Westminster Abbey or the lay community in Lambeth Palace. Projected community relations are also omnipresent through Facebook groups, professional associations or pressure groups.

And can we go further than talking about the architecture of a community – who is in it? How is it formed? What purpose does it serve? – and also talk about what it feels like from the inside, its inner life, which is a qualitative measure. How do you create a sense of community? That sense of community is located in its common purpose, emotional connections and ability to influence. Community *per se* is nothing if it has no traction, no sense of engagement and draw. Nor should we ignore the significance of the integration of needs, that is to say, the establishment of a common purpose, whether a community project gathered around preserving a local wildlife area or the rambling club that meets each Monday morning. And inevitably, that creates a shared emotional connection; after all, this is not a business transaction or commercial exchange, this is about life investment.

Organic growth of community

It is worth reminding ourselves that community is not a static given, delivered as it were fully formed. It is organic, historically active and continually developing. If one reflects briefly on the development of the monastic movement, it soon becomes apparent how rich a tapestry was woven for centuries, long before St Benedict ever came on the scene in the sixth century.

St Anthony in the third century is usually considered the father of all monks, but in fact was an ascetic, a hermit. Others had retreated to the outskirts of civilization, to the fringes of cities, but Anthony is notable for having decided to go beyond that tradition and head out into the desert proper. He left for the Nitrian Desert on the edge of the Western Desert about 60 miles west of Alexandria, where he remained for 13 years. When he attempted to live a solitary and reflective existence away from the temptations of the world, the flesh and the devil, what he found was that it was his inner demons that needed combatting and that he was overwhelmed by the number of those who came from the cities seeking his advice.

Communal monasticism proper – living in community – began with St Pachomius the Great who established his first monastery between 318 and 323 at Tabennisi, Egypt. His elder brother John joined him, and soon more than 100 monks lived nearby. St Pachomius set about turning these cells into a formal organization. Until then, Christian asceticism had been solitary or *eremitic*: monastics lived in individual huts or caves and met only occasionally for worship. St Pachomius created the community or *cenobitic* organization in which monastics lived together and held their property in common under the leadership of an abbot or abbess.

In the west in about the year 500, St Benedict gave up his studies in Rome, at age 14, and chose the life of an ascetic monk in the pursuit of personal holiness, living as a hermit in a cave near the rugged region of Subiaco. In time, he too began to attract disciples and after considerable initial struggles with his first community at Subiaco, he eventually founded the monastery of Monte Cassino in 529, where he wrote his Rule. This Rule of Life heralded a truly communal form of living, an interdependent community. If we say that the pre-Reformation community in Westminster Abbey was the daughter of Monte Cassino, then we may even dare to describe the post-Reformation Elizabethan foundation we now have as its grandchild.

In other words, while we might imagine we can draw a direct line from St Anthony in the desert of Egypt in the third century right through to the current post-Reformation foundation in Westminster, we should not pretend that these are remotely the same things. We could call each of them 'communities' in a religious sense, but each one has developed and responded to particular social, political and environmental pressures to create unique ecologies.

The communities of Westminster and Whitehall

Having set out some theoretical frameworks to help us understand and interpret what we mean by 'community', I want in this final section to explore what kind of 'communities' exist here in Westminster and Whitehall and to consider what impact the lasting imprint of the monastic community and their successors might have on those of us who live and work here.

If we begin with Westminster Abbey and use the three filters I described earlier, it is possible, I think, to come to an understanding of what kind of community now exists within that iconic building. The filters I suggested were:

- community *versus* society

- grounded, lifestyle or projected communities

- a sense of community created by membership, influence, common purpose and shared emotional connection.

It is evident to me that at its very heart, a religious establishment has to be a *community* rather than a *society*; it must be *Gemeinschaft* rather than *Gesellschaft*, not least because if it were *Gesellschaft* it would teeter on the verge of theocracy. While Christianity may once have laid claim to societal powers in western Europe, the Reformation and Enlightenment eras have modified our basic belief that such a thing is now possible or indeed desirable.

While many who now work at Westminster Abbey do so simply, and rightly, as a means of employment, its core purpose as a religious community continues to be in relation to deeply held beliefs, morals and conformity to a pattern of living. As Tönnies described it, this is a community based on feelings of togetherness and on mutual bonds, which are felt as a goal to be sought, with its members being the means to reach this goal.

Without doubt, there is a strong element in Westminster Abbey of a lifestyle community: a community formed around a clear set of beliefs and practices, in this case religious ones. However, there is another equally significant facet to be recognized here, as it often is in parish churches, namely that of geography, the second filter. While we might want to argue that a religious establishment is primarily about beliefs, practices and values – the bonds of a common lifestyle – it is undoubtedly the case that 'location, location, location' is equally important. If we think back to AD 960 and St Dunstan's act as Bishop of London in granting precisely this plot of land to the Benedictines of Glastonbury, that one act of patronage has had enormous – and unforeseen – consequences for the formation of the English, and later British, state.

Nor is it difficult to use the third filter, that of 'a sense of community', to interpret what is going on here. The current community may not quite use the rigorous, year-long testing to prove the sincerity of canons or lay members of the Abbey, but it has its modern-day equivalent in the interview process conducted in the Jerusalem Chamber. Influence, common purpose and shared emotional connections are all things readily identifiable in the life of the Abbey.

So far so good: I am arguing that Westminster Abbey is a community based on lifestyle with a heavy geographical element and a sense of community reinforced by influence, common purpose and shared connections.

But what about Whitehall and the 'Westminster Village'? Can we describe them as communities in a way that is useful, illuminating or helpful, and if so, what are their characteristics? Further, how has the foundation stone of a religious community left its mark?

Within the walls of Westminster Abbey, 'Parliament Square' is used as a shorthand to describe the four sides of the square as a metaphor for British public life – the legislature in the Palace of Westminster, the judiciary in the Supreme Court, the government departments in Whitehall with the faith community completing the fourth side of the square. It would be easy to think of these simply as instruments of *Gesellschaft*, society. These institutions serve to maintain the equilibrium of society through legislation, police, courts and prisons. It is about the creation of a nationally agreed set of parameters by which the citizen can, without prejudice or interference, pursue his or her own aims and goals. But over and above all these societal elements, I want to highlight what I think are three community-like aspects that shape both the culture and practice of Whitehall: geography, ethos and vocation.

Even if we cannot properly speak of these departments as separate 'communities', it is clear that geography also has an important role to play. Many functions of government have rightly been outsourced far beyond London, for example, with the Driver and Vehicle Licensing Agency (DVLA) in Swansea. But the core business of engaging with the legislature is still focused around a remarkably small plot of land.

So St Dunstan has left his mark. And at their very best, government departments aspire to some of those kite-marks, if I can put it that way, of community: membership, influence, common purpose and shared emotional connection. The geographical positioning of the Government Department a stone's throw away from the Palace of Westminster or from Downing Street reinforces a physical sense of community. And one of the most striking reflections for me, as a Whitehall and Westminster outsider, is the very strong sense of culture evident in the individual institutions. Indeed, some will have a fully articulated story, a narrative by which they express both their past history and their current objectives.

But second, alongside this geographical element, it is noteworthy that the Institute for Government's report *Ministers Reflect: On Parliament* (Hughes and White 2016) talked about the disjuncture experienced by politicians moving into ministerial roles, being faced by what they perceived as civil servants who in some cases seemed not to understand the culture of Parliament nor the pressures they were facing as individuals. The former Immigration Minister, Damian Green, was quoted as saying that '[Parliament] is almost the only medium in which you can lose your job in about half an hour and a lot of officials don't get that at all' Hughes and White 2016, (p.1). And, I suspect, misapprehension and miscomprehension is a two-way street: many civil servants will be bemused by elected politicians who seem not to 'get it'. In other words, each department and institution has developed its own very strong ethos and culture, a form of socialization in itself, which is to a greater or lesser extent acknowledged and conscious.

And the third point I want to make returns me to the opening section of my essay, taken from Chapter 58 of the Rule of St Benedict. I set out there in some detail the lengthy and laborious process by which a postulant had to persevere, metaphorically and literally banging on the door of the monastery to gain entrance, then spending a year having the Rule read to them over and over again, weighing up the cost of their decision, before finally taking vows of stability, conversion of manners and obedience, being stripped of their goods and garments and then clothed in their new garb.

There is no easy read-across with the formation of a public servant, but undoubtedly the process of becoming a civil servant involves an element of socialization and for many the impact is profound. The Nolan Principles of Public Service are fundamental to the modern British state: selflessness, integrity, objectivity, accountability, openness, honesty and leadership. Anyone involved in even a modest level of enculturation will recognize that these are core dispositions that do not happen by themselves, but rather require the intentional engagement of the institutions as formative communities. For many in public service, we might even speak of a sense of vocation.

So the point I am making is that while we are not at all surprised to find strong community characteristics in Westminster Abbey, we might perhaps be startled to find them present in the departments and institutions that are so prominent in our public life and political discourse. Indeed, we might even say that Parliament Square occupies an intermediate and intermediary space between society and community.

Conclusion

In this essay, I began with a description of 'community' as the ecology in which virtues and aspirations can flourish. The novice entering a monastic house underwent fundamental change both in his or her behaviour – committing to a rigorous and unbending lifestyle – and in his or her 'virtues' – taking vows of stability, the conversion of morals and obedience. Beyond the individual, the history of monastic communities, itself the foundation stone for the creation of Westminster, shows how these communities have developed under different social environments and have grown organically.

The theoretical frameworks available for describing how different communities operate help us both to locate Westminster Abbey as a religious community within its peculiar ecology and to understand how the institutions of government, which have grown up on Thorney Island over the last millennium, display many of the characteristics of communities through their geography, ethos and socialization.

However, we should not impose a contemporary distinction between religion and politics on our pre-modern forebears. This brief extract from a history of the Abbey (Page 1909) recounts the re-founding of the Abbey by St Edward the Confessor in 1065:

> This is sober history: legend again intervening tells how Edward, having subdued his kingdom, vowed a pilgrimage to Rome to return thanks for his success, but was absolved by the pope at the instigation of the English nobles, who feared for the hard-won safety of the realm if the king were to go abroad. The condition of the absolution was that Edward should build or restore a monastery in honour of St Peter, but before the bishops bearing the message had returned to England, a hermit, Wilsinus by name, sought the king, and told him that the prince of the apostles had appeared to him in a dream foretelling the return of the ambassadors and pointing out the ancient monastery of Thorney as the spot where he wished his church to stand.

Or, to put it another way, the creation of the monastic community, the forerunner of all religious, royal and political life in Westminster, was not simply a religious act in the narrow, privatized way that we might suppose. It took place within the historic context of the defence of the realm and was part of a broader political narrative around maintaining political stability in a time of extreme flux and disturbance.

In the uncertainties of our own days, that seems good and timely to remember.

THE CONVERSION OF MANNERS

Claire Foster-Gilbert

Introduction: monastic virtues

A novice monk was sent to the library of his monastery to
learn the art of manuscript copying from the senior monks.
He sat industriously at his carrel, trying to form his letters as
beautifully as those he was copying. His script was the law
of his monastery and he could not help but notice that the
manuscript from which he was working was itself a copy.
He asked the Abbot, with some trepidation, if it might not
be the case that the copies from which the monks were
copying might contain some mistakes, which would then
be perpetuated. The Abbot thought he had a point and
disappeared off to the dark dungeons of the Abbey to find
the originals.

He was gone for hours, and then eventually discovered,
covered in dungeon dust, clutching a manuscript, in floods
of tears. 'It doesn't say celibate,' he said. 'It says celebrate.'

In 1912 Cuthbert Butler, a real monk who became Abbot
of Downside, discovered that for a thousand years Benedictine
monks had been faithfully and wrongly copying a phrase in
the Rule of St Benedict, the phrase that is translated into

English as 'conversion of manners'. *Conversio moro* was in fact *conversatio moro*. Unlike the difference between 'celibate' and 'celebrate', however, the distinction between the two Latin forms was not clear. Indeed, the phrase, whether *conversio* or *conversatio*, is not clear, and debate amongst scholars as to what Benedict might have meant by it continues.

The phrase 'conversion of manners' is the rough translation of the third of the three vows Benedictines make, the first two being stability and obedience. The vows are found in the Rule of St Benedict, which dates back to the sixth century.

Benedict's Rule and the form of monasticism that it founded signified a change in the way the religious life was led. Hitherto it had centred upon following one holy and charismatic person into the desert; now communities were created who, together, placed themselves under a rule of life. But the core monastic virtue was not lost. Centred in the practice of Christ himself, who withdrew regularly to barren places to pray, the monk or nun made the choice to enter the metaphorical desert. For Irish monks the desert was the sea, and their little coracles washed up on the unforgiving rocky shores of the Skellig Islands. Others simply left the city. Still others located themselves in the heart of the city. To 'enter the desert' was to renounce the addictions that make up a human life and throw oneself at the mercy of God to provide. The extremism this engendered in some earnest religious souls, such as the lonely ascetics on Skellig St Michael, was tempered by Benedict's rule of moderation, which allowed a little wine and some sensible husbandry into the desert community, and this has stood the test of time, contributing in no small manner, and somewhat ironically, to the wealth of western Europe. There are thriving Benedictine communities today and, although numbers are down, there is some evidence of a revival of interest in 'entering the desert'.

The vow *conversatio moro* can be understood thus. The Latin word *conversatio* carries the sense of 'change or turn with', and *moro* is the basis of the word 'mores', our morals, our social norms and customs, those ideas and perceptions from which our behaviour springs. The monks of the Community of the Resurrection at Mirfield, an Anglican order following the Benedictine Rule, say they understand their vow of conversion of morals to be one of turning again towards God, choosing the metaphorical desert, every day. Patrick Mark Hederman, Benedictine Abbot of Glenstal in Limerick, writes that the vow can be experienced as undergoing a 'cultural conversion', surrendering the addictive ideas or mores that govern our behaviour in order to become what God wants us to be. The metaphorical desert is a place of not owning anything, including knowledge.

Conversion of manners today

In this essay, I will explore the vow 'conversion of manners', a vow that has been life-giving to Benedictine communities for 15 centuries. I will consider it as a virtue that is relevant to the communities of public servants who operate in Parliament Square, around the thousand-year-old Benedictine foundation of Westminster Abbey, with the hope that it might be of some use to them.

My method, borrowed from that remarkable twentieth-century philosopher Paul Ricoeur, is this: if we have an ancient concept that has remained meaningful and regenerative to communities of people for a very long time, then it is worth asking it to offer meaning and regeneration to our situation today. What I want to do in this essay is not to delve deeply into the past for understanding, but to delve deeply into our needy present for questions that the concept might help to answer. 'Conversion of manners', however understood, has passed the test of time, so I want it to work hard to serve the tests of our time. Specifically, I want to bring it to the question that fundamentally underlies the work of the people and institutions around Parliament Square, which is, 'what is the good that we should be trying to do?'

How does 'conversion of manners' help answer the question 'what is the good that we should be trying to do?'? Conversion of manners, with its sense of daily returning and retuning, implies that goodness is not binary. The returning and retuning to the good that we seek means both facing the complexities and contradictions that arise in context and taking steps to protect ourselves against the pressures that corrupt, corrode and confound our seeking and staying with the good.

Christianity, in common with other faiths, has an understanding of conversion as a second birth, experienced as a moment of decision, after which nothing is the same. I still remember the slightly queasy feeling I had when a former Bishop of Liverpool fixed me with a gimlet eye over breakfast at the Athenaeum and asked me when I became a Christian, and I really knew that 'when I was christened as a baby' was the wrong answer. (We were meant to be discussing environmental issues, so it seemed a rather irrelevant and frankly impertinent question, especially at breakfast.) What I should have said was: I'm still becoming one. The first conversion is the enemy of the second, Bishop, because when you convert you think you have found the truth and that blinds you to further truth and understanding.

Shifting paradigms

What, though, might conversion look like, outside the specifically religious sphere? There are times in our lives, in the lives of our communities, our workplaces and society more generally, when new realizations dawn and things change. The biggest changes happen when there is a paradigm shift, and this might be thought of as the ultimate conversion of manners. A paradigm shift comes about because of a discovery that looks like nothing we have seen before. It requires an openness to seeing completely new possibilities and a willingness to try new ways of making them happen. The story of penicillin is a good example. Alexander Fleming took ten years to understand the implications of the mould he saw growing in a petri dish in his laboratory, because he was certain, as everyone was at the time, that infection could not be treated systemically but only topically, if at all. The possibility that one might swallow a tablet and this would deal with infection anywhere in the body was simply not a possibility his mind entertained, so he did not see it. Once he did, and once, crucially, the multidisciplinary team had been brought together by Walter Florey to create the medicine, everything changed. But we notice now, 60 years on, how serious a problem we have of over-use of antibiotics. We have inherited the paradigm that you can treat infection with a pill, and the pharmaceutical industry has enjoyed half a century's golden age predicated on that belief. Now we are failing to understand that we may not, after all, be able to treat infection with a pill if the infection is a bacterium that has subsequently learned to circumvent the properties of the pill. All the time we fail to see that, we continue to take antibiotics because it always used to work, we think, so why should it not still? Lives are endangered by our drug-taking habit, as over-use of antibiotics increases the number of superbugs and infection can no longer be treated. Pharmaceuticals are not the magical bullets we once thought, with good reason, they were. The first conversion (paradigm shift) is the enemy of the second.

A similar trajectory can be seen in our perception of, and beliefs about, energy sources. The capacity of coal and oil for producing energy was discovered, ways were found to harness the energy and a paradigm shift ensued in the form of the industrial revolution, with all its immense benefits…and now, as we know, its immense disbenefits to the atmosphere. Today, the addiction to that way of seeing, that way of living, is preventing the next paradigm shift into resourcing energy needs in a less harmful way.

And so with change within ourselves. We are heading in one direction, light dawns that it is the wrong direction and we head with enthusiasm in a different direction, unable or unwilling to listen for contradictory voices, wrapped in the zeal of our own certainty. And perhaps, if the shift in our belief system is profound enough and counter-cultural enough, we have to be focused and single minded for a bit. But woe betide us, especially leaders, if we fail to pay attention to disagreement. It is especially important for leaders, because human beings are susceptible, and we rather like having someone who tells us with great certainty what we should believe. We can heave the responsibility on to that person, give him the glory if he wants it (which he usually does) and also the blame when it all goes wrong. We, meanwhile, were only obeying orders.

Jeffrey Sachs writes that J. F. Kennedy employed someone whose sole task was to disagree with him (Sachs 2013). J. F. Kennedy had a personal devil's advocate, because he recognized that once you reach a certain level of seniority you will be surrounded by yeasayers. The professor, judge, bishop, director general in the civil service, general in the army, dean and commander in the police deliberately (because they think that is what leadership is) or inadvertently switch their tuner button permanently to 'transmit' and it never goes back to 'receive' unless it is intentionally retuned. No one is going to ask you to do that: you have to know you must do it yourself. The Institute's Fellows' programme enrols public servants at the level not too far below this one, in order to prepare them to listen for disagreement when no one will be asking them to. It is the idea behind the fool or jester at court. Abbot Patrick Mark writes of the importance in the religious life of the *anam cara*, roughly translated as spiritual friend, who will watch over your addictive tendencies and tell you the truth. Martin Donnelly, a senior civil servant with long experience, defined a good leader as 'one who seeks counsel'. And thank heavens for a free press, for the media, too, will prevent messianic tendencies.

Moreover, it is the willingness to listen to disagreement that will create the open mindset that makes seeing differently possible, seeing the things that we cannot now see. It should be noted that utilitarianism does not like this. Utilitarianism, which uses numbers to come to moral conclusions, likes certainties. You can only put a number against something that you know exists. If you have not yet seen it, you cannot count it. In this regard, Iain McGilchrist (2009) contrasts the Romantics favourably with the rationalist Kant, and Bentham, father of utilitarianism. McGilchrist cites Wordsworth, 'Listening intently for the call of the owl, I hear the sound of mountain torrents' (McGilchrist 2009, p.376). The Romantics took their walks in twilight, open to the mystery of nature and the universe. Kant and Bentham, by contrast, took their walks (not together, of course) in full daylight and always at the same time each day, so reliably that people set their watches by them. Abbot Patrick Mark suggests the Benedictine vow of obedience means 'to listen', and Sister Joan Chittister says that this is to become 'an ear that pays attention to every single thing the universe is saying' (Chittister 2010, p.75, first published 1992). Esther de Waal equates listening with humility, which shares a root with humus, leaf mould that dies and breaks down and from which new life can grow (de Waal 1999, p.29, first published 1984). Listening to disagreement makes you more likely to acknowledge that you do not, in the end, know. Returning to the desert is reconnecting with not knowing, out of which new perceptions can then arise.

Mostly, though, we do not want to listen to disagreement because it is actually very hard to accept mutually incompatible moral claims or arguments that are simultaneously true and inconsistent with each other. But we need to be able to wait with paradox rather than reach too quickly for our benefit–cost ratio calculators. The 2010 film *Of Gods and Men* told the true story of a group of monks in Algeria at the time of the civil war. Hitherto the monks had lived in good harmony with their Muslim neighbours; now they were threatened with extermination by extremists unless they left. Should they stay or should they go? They were after all providing important medical care to the villagers. And yet staying meant mortal danger. But when the question was put to the vote the oldest monk said, 'I don't know yet.' His 'sacred stubbornness' might be thought of as a luxury in a monastery where there is time, but those Algerian monks did not have much time.

A tennis player has even less. I commend to you the Andy Murray principle of decision-making. The longer he left his decision about how to play his return shot as the ball was coming at him from his opponent, the better the decision would be, because the longer he left it, the more information he had about the trajectory of the ball, the position of his opponent and any other contextual data that would be relevant to the success of his return move. Milliseconds made a difference.

I had a kind of conversion experience some two years after coming to Westminster Abbey to set up the Institute. In those two years, I had immersed myself in the culture of public service and made friends with some of the people doing it. My conversion was to the perception of a deep level of uncorruption around Parliament Square. The Institute, I saw, was not to be founded upon a narrative of crisis. Westminster and Whitehall were not 'all wrong' and its people were not 'all bad'. But this perception has to be questioned: I have to be like Karl Popper's good scientist: one who will try to disprove her hypothesis, not, as is the tendency, to see data to support it wherever she looks. The first conversion opens our eyes to new realities, but then we only see those new realities. Only penicillin will prevent infection. Only coal and oil will give us energy. I have indeed been finding that I only meet wonderfully uncorrupt public servants and I only notice the institutional mechanisms that support uncorruption. So I read *How Corrupt is Britain?* by David Whyte (2015), who claims to demonstrate profound corruption at senior levels in the establishment. His method is to expose what he sees as the evil of neo-liberal capitalism:

What we have been witnessing over the past 30 years has been the systematic erosion of this public realm as more and more of the public sector has been privatized, outsourced, or made subject to market principles. It is this process that has led to the long list of abuses catalogued [in the book]. Is it any wonder that ministers, civil servants and military leaders should expect to use their office as a means of leveraging fat jobs in the private sector when those they rub shoulders with on a daily basis are doing the same in their own business sphere? (Whyte 2015, p.45)

David Whyte has an agenda, but that does not make him wrong, and I hear him, though I really do not want to believe that the public servants I work with and the friends I have made would be so corrupt. I don't want to believe it of myself. The really valuable point is that we are all vulnerable to corruption and no matter how relatively uncorrupt the system is, it is, and we are, never uncorruptible. My conversion to championing uncorruption in Parliament Square is tempered, now, by a recognition of the forces that corrode it. They are not just financial. Power has a corrosive force all of its own. A politician must first of all seek and retain power, must be selected, elected and re-elected. Power is her fuel and there is never enough to go around. She can only change the world if she has power, and seeking power will change her. Being in the public eye, essential to the politician seeking office, is also corrosive. Hannah Arendt (1998, p.74, first published 1958) goes so far as to assert that goodness cannot survive publicity. A person can be great, or he can be good. He cannot be both.

Moral challenges in public service

Let us now look at the question 'what good should we be trying to do?' through the prism of conversion of manners in some specific contexts around Parliament Square. Senior civil servant Clare Moriarty wrote some years ago about the inherent values conflict for the civil servant. Civil servants are, generally speaking, idealistic people with very deep and lasting public service values. Moriarty identifies these as a motivation to want to make the world a better place to live in, tempered by realism and guardianship of propriety. These values describe the good that civil servants believe they should do and are powerful motivators for their work. And yet by the nature of the political system we have, and indeed in service to the democratic principle, civil servants must adopt and make work not their own values but those of the minister whom they serve, without necessarily sharing or even understanding them. Moriarty writes:

> Some core values appear to be shared. Idealism is a strong value for politicians as it is for civil servants. But for a party politician it is perhaps axiomatic that the world will be a better place to live in if their party is in government and therefore able to implement the policies to which it is committed...
>
> Civil servants don't aspire to be politicians. We would be in the wrong job if we did: that much is contained in the fundamental tenet of civil service neutrality. So we clearly shouldn't be internalising political value systems – but we effectively have to live by them. The oddity in the civil service 'deal' is not that political values prevail...but that, of everyone in [a government department], only ministers and their special advisers are expected to subscribe to

those values. And the fear of compromising political neutrality means that there is little incentive…to understand the political value system, and indeed some subtle discouragement from doing so. (Moriarty 2006, pp.1–2)

The inherent conflict keeps the civil servant in a state of continued questioning and, at its best, allows him to remain open in precisely the way I have been arguing 'conversion of manners' means. But it is important he understands that the moral conflict is inherent and healthy, otherwise he may think his discomfort implies there is something wrong. This will affect leadership in the civil service, because values are so vital to the motivation and uncorrupt behaviour of the civil servant.

Here is what it looks like from the other side, the side of the politician. Gerald Kaufman writes in his book *How to be a Minister*:

What Whitehall does believe in, for better or for worse, is continuity… It is not, 'Do I agree with it?' but 'Can I make it work?' [The civil servants] may not agree with you politically…but they really do have a sense of loyalty to their ministers… It is very easy and rather unpleasant to have rows with people who in the nature of things cannot answer you back. (Kaufman 1997, p.35, first published 1980)

If you are looking for ideas for legislation, Kaufman says, do not turn to your civil servants but to your party's election programme. He details the navigation of your (party's) ideas from manifesto through legislation to policy implementation, via the civil service system, through Parliament, without antagonizing MPs who have to defend you locally or the national party membership, and then back to the civil service machine again. The journey is complex and exhausting, and at every step of the way compromising adjustments have to be made to ensure safe passage of your bill. But you must attend to these different constituencies or suffer the misery that they will make of your life. And you must never forget that you and your party will need to be re-elected. If you do not have power, you do not have anything.

At their best, the navigation challenges for the politician demand that she attend to different views, and her 'conversion of manners' is sustained by constant reference to her communities. But the challenges will also whittle away at her good intentions and the good intentions of her policies. She is in danger of acting only as a people pleaser and not as a leader. The power she must always attend to retaining will corrode her aim to make the world a better place unless she consciously takes steps to protect herself.

Another hot arena for moral dilemmas in public life is experienced by Westminster Abbey's near neighbours the Metropolitan Police. The London Policing Ethics Panel, chaired by the formidably analytical Lord Carlile, published a report entitled *Ethical Challenges of Policing in London*, in which the following observation was made:

> Because they hold public authority, the public tends to expect police officers to be exemplars of morality. That is, the public expects the police to be ethically better than the rest of us. Yet we have also seen that police officers must regularly make quick judgements in applying abstract concepts to challenging situations. The police will face more ethical dilemmas than most of us, where something bad will unavoidably happen. And when they make mistakes these will often have larger-than-normal impacts on people's lives. So the very people who we expect to be ethically better than us will in fact do more things that are

harmful and wrong – just because that is the nature of their
job. (London Policing Ethics Panel 2014, p.12)

Police officers have to respond, often very quickly, to
extremely complicated situations where the moral issues at
stake are manifold and conflicting. A moral philosopher can
take a lifetime to unpick the dilemmas; a police officer has to
act fast to limit damage and bring criminals to justice. Called
to a potential crime scene, she will need speedily to weigh
in the balance any combination of any number of: drug or
alcohol addiction, sexual, emotional or physical abuse, familial
neglect, poverty, bad housing, bad schooling and mental
illness. The Andy Murray approach to decision-making
applies: make your decision and act decisively, but make it as
late as is safely possible, because there is so much to see and
try to understand in the making of it.

For the one running a police force the competing moral
imperatives are also manifold. Criminals must be brought to
justice but the process of so doing must be fair. The moral
imperative is that no one should be condemned without
fair trial. At the same time, victims must be confident that
if they come forward to speak, they will be heard. There is
a fraught hinterland here particularly in the world of abuse,
born of attitudes and beliefs about women and children in
particular – that they are not to be trusted and believed, that
they do not believe they will be trusted and believed and that
the relationships within which abuse takes place are such
that they do not know if they even believe themselves. The
victim can harbour devastating feelings of responsibility
for the wrong that has been done, confusing the case and
making clarity and truth that much harder to reach. There
can be a crazy notion in the victim's mind of needing to

protect the abuser. The knowledge of deep-down, hidden, shameful memories that any of us who have taken time for therapy or confession know about, hidden, suppressed and doubted, confound truth. There is a moral imperative, owed to victims and to truth itself, to work hard to find the reality of the situation.

There is the moral imperative not to act on the word of someone who has made false accusations. In the midst of the clouds of uncertainty that beset the victim's situation, how is the false accusation to be weeded out? And yet it must be, because it is also a moral imperative to avoid damage to the falsely accused.

There is the moral imperative for forgiveness and reconciliation, vital to the health of people who must be able to move on. Those who harbour bitterness and resentment and cannot lay them to rest become warped in their perceptions and lost to society because until the hurt is addressed they cannot be of service to others. To whom are apologies owed? When are apologies morally demanded? Do too many of them devalue the currency? Righteous indignation on behalf of others is easy, much easier than righteous indignation on our own behalves, but perhaps that's why we should have it – to defend each other, to protect each other's reputations if we are diffident about defending our own.

Conclusion

'What is the good we should be trying to do?' is answered, by the Benedictine virtue conversion of manners, as openness not only to the great paradigm shifts, the great conversions to new perceptions and beliefs, but also a daily openness to counterfactuals, to apparently opposing truths, to the data that do not demonstrate the truth of your hypotheses. Conversion of manners is cultivating a character that can withstand corrosion but remains open to difference. It is growing the strength and courage to wait with contradiction until it is necessary to decide and act.

I believe, not because I think I should, but rather as a matter of disposition, that the reason we can and should look for what we cannot now see, and wait with fortitude in the face of paradox and inconsistency, not for solutions, but rather for clarity about the next step towards goodness, is that there *is* goodness. I am, then, in sympathy with this poem by another great figure from the sixth century, Boethius, which encourages us to hold fast to what we feel to be true and always listen for more:

> This discord in the pact of things,
> This endless war twixt truth and truth,
> That singly hold, yet give the lie
> To him who seeks to yoke them both-
> ...
> And therefore whoso seeks the truth
> Shall find in no wise peace of heart.
> For neither does he wholly know,
> And neither doth he all forget:
> But that high thing which once he saw,
> And still remembers, that he holds,
> And seeks to bring the truth forgot
> Again to that which he has yet.

The following is one of the best conversion stories I have heard recently. A tourist from China came up to one of Westminster Abbey's beadles (security guards) and said, 'I've just been in the Abbey, and I saw a statue of the Virgin Mary.

So is the Abbey Catholic?' The beadle replied, 'It was Catholic until 1531, after which it was Anglican.' He then saw the tourist go to his wife and explain to her that the Abbey was Catholic until half past three and then it becomes Anglican.

Reflections

―――――○―――――――――――――――――――○―――――

Timeliness and Timelessness

Peter Hennessy in Conversation with Claire Foster-Gilbert

This conversation was recorded in November 2016, just as the High Court was ruling that Parliament had to authorize Britain's withdrawal from the European Union and Donald Trump was being elected as the President of the United States. Peter Hennessy, in conversation with Claire Foster-Gilbert, reflects on the themes of the foregoing essays, testing their value in the light of current events.

CLAIRE FOSTER-GILBERT

What reflections overall do you have on the essays in the book?

PETER HENNESSY

There are two golden threads running through the book. One is the Benedictine notion of stability. Never has our country, in its public and political life, needed more a sound like that to emanate from these extraordinary walls of Westminster Abbey. What we are facing is not just Brexit itself, it is what Brexit has shown us about who we are. George Orwell would see a country as an extended family. Our extended family, these islands, is one that has ceased to know itself and we have ceased to know each other within that self. The EU referendum was a lightning flash to illuminate this landscape that had long been in the changing. And it has disturbed people. Quite apart from the uncertainty in our geopolitical position, the UK has now become a destabilizing force in the world. That is not how we have seen ourselves: in living memory we have been quite the reverse. That in turn has destabilized the way we see ourselves. These destabilizers mean that a clear view and song of stability amidst anxiety is wonderfully timely. The Europe within which Benedict wrote his Rule for monastic life was unstable: he wanted islands of serenity and stability within seas of absolute insecurity and instability. That is the enduring sound. It is your phrase, Claire, that the Abbey is porous to the other institutions around the Square and indeed to the country more widely. It is the porosity of Westminster Abbey through its Institute that is very special. So many of the essay writers in this volume have touched on that in different ways.

Second, there is a thread of recognition of how tricky it is in the modern world to talk about ethics and morality in our public and political life without sounding preachy. I can understand why; there is a tremendous temptation to preach heavier than our weight in the world, particularly when we haven't other ways of influencing the world. It's an imperial overhang. The sort of people who preach heavier than their weight in the world would shudder at the thought that they might be part of a post-imperial legacy. But the

British Empire was a preaching organization as well as an administrative one. That bit carries on and the rest of the world can get quite irritated by us, the superior Brits.

CLAIRE FOSTER-GILBERT

So is William Hague wrong in his call to this country to wake up the conscience of the world and keep it restless?

PETER HENNESSY

The restless conscience is a wonderful idea. Hague is not wrong. But you have to apply it carefully and sparingly otherwise you devalue that conscience. Then the restlessness just sounds like preaching and interference of the worst kind. Hague was certainly onto something and the restless conscience at times in our history has woken up the world. We think of the example of slavery, and there are many other examples.

CLAIRE FOSTER-GILBERT

Hague is particularly concerned with sexual violence in conflict.

PETER HENNESSY

That's something you should never leave alone; there are no caveats on saying what you think about that. It is the overall preachiness that we need to avoid, because it can all too often sound as though we are asking 'why can't the rest of the world be more like us?' We have to watch that tendency, particularly when the rest of the world is quite cross with us, certainly the rest of the European Union is, because of all the trouble we are causing.

CLAIRE FOSTER-GILBERT

How then is moral leadership shown? What is the tone of voice? The experience of Westminster Abbey Institute is that politicians in particular are wary of coming anywhere near the words morality or ethics, and civil servants too, in a different way, because they think they have to keep their morality out of the way in order to serve the government of the day. But we want to show that being moral means exercising that muscle, just as one might go to the gym regularly for physical exercise, so one needs to exercise and keep one's moral sensibility healthy.

PETER HENNESSY

Yes. We need to think of how things could be and strive mightily to make them so, as in the example of sexual violence in conflict. We should follow Abraham Lincoln's beautiful call in his inaugural speech, with the Civil War about to erupt, when he said we should appeal to the better angels of people's natures. Even in the most frightful regimes in the world, there are people of conscience and sensitivity, sometimes even within the regimes themselves and not just suppressed within the country.

So we have to find the tone of voice and indeed the vocabulary to work on the better angels of people's nature without sounding as if we are bossing them or being superior. It's very tricky to pull that off, and that's why it has to be rationed and not indiscriminate.

There's something else we need to do, and this advice comes from Sir Tom Phillips, former ambassador. Tom told me that one of the rules of diplomatic life, when he was accredited to a country for the first time, not just as an ambassador but when he was a junior diplomat too, was to find out what activity of that country's national life the people of that country are the least self-aware about. And when we apply it to our own county, we find it's this preaching above our weight – and also punching above our weight in the world. We have an appetite to cut a bit of a dash, not just to be a medium-sized power, a former world power, who is going through a bit of a difficult patch with the neighbours at the moment. There is more to it than that. It's what we don't see. Some would say we're an amazingly self-aware nation but no nation is fully self-aware.

CLAIRE FOSTER-GILBERT

Nor is any person.

PETER HENNESSY

So we need to become aware of the angels of our nature as well as other people's, and our collective natures in terms of international organizations. I'm very sympathetic to Hague's very good line about the restless conscience but you do have to be careful.

Westminster Abbey Institute has an even finer line to tread because it is faith based, and that cannot be denied: the very stones bespeak a thousand years of worship here, through thick and thin. This Abbey has endured through the vicissitudes of the nation, as a pool of solace, a classic Benedictine artefact. The Institute has to be careful, in its porosity to other institutions, especially secular state institutions, that it doesn't appear to be the Anglican Church, carefully camouflaged, putting itself about.

CLAIRE FOSTER-GILBERT

The truth is that the Institute bends over so far backwards trying *not* to preach that people wonder who we are. They wonder why they are sitting in a church talking about deep moral questions. We don't articulate where we are coming from very well, because we don't want to proselytize.

PETER HENNESSY

That is one of the great strengths of the Anglican tradition. There is part of it that loves proselytizing, but the Abbey cannot be accused of that. This moral leadership is not done by leading by example either. It's more gentle, asking, 'Have you thought about this? Because if you have, we have one or two thoughts we might share, because we think the real problems are here and here. Let's talk about it.' And that is far more effective than becoming a clerical management consultancy, whose aim is change and which offers five bullet points of things you've got to do to transform. The transformation agenda. Dear oh dear, we have quite enough of that in business life.

CLAIRE FOSTER-GILBERT

If we have an agenda, it is simply this: think more deeply about the good you're trying to do. Believe that you, or at any rate a big part of you, seeks the good and wants goodness to be made more manifest in the world.

PETER HENNESSY

Well that's absolutely fine. The public service impulse is very strong in this country and is represented in the other bits of the state around Parliament Square, the judiciary, the Home and Foreign Civil Service and the Diplomatic Service, the Houses of Parliament, both of them. Although the sceptical public sometimes thinks the public service impulse can be turned into something self-serving. The public are not entirely throbbing with undiluted admiration for public servants or politicians at the moment. They never are, really, but at the moment they're certainly not. But the public service impulse and the notion of Crown Service, to put it in the British constitutional context, is both a deep and a wonderful thing.

The senior civil servants in the government departments who have had to manage the relationship with the EU in its various forms have been doing so for 43 years. There are not many now serving who were there in the days when we were first coming in to the EU with the 1972 Act and the 1973 Accession, but a considerable number of them have spent the bulk of their working lives making that relationship work and keeping the show on the road. It has struck me how hard it must be to act on proper instructions from duly appointed ministers to dismantle something you have been mantling, so to speak, for the bulk of your professional life. It is your duty to do what you've been instructed to do, while of course always explaining caveats and the difficulties, but nevertheless dismantling this relationship you have been working on and with all these years. It must be so difficult to spend the day doing that and to go home with your private thoughts.

There is a comparison with the generation I first wrote about when I was a Whitehall Correspondent in the early 1970s. This was the generation that had come back from the War, mainly male, not entirely but mainly, that's changed thank goodness. This generation was involved in

the reconstruction of the country after the War. There had
been no recruitment to it during the War, so they had to
cram them all in over two or three years, brought in under
the so-called reconstruction competitions, these people who
had been in the Forces. They were an extraordinary group
of people, because of what they had seen and done before
they were 25. They'd grown up in the slump of the 1930s and
been in the War, and one of them, Ian Bancroft, went on to
be Head of the Home Civil Service, a lovely man. He said,
'We were the generation for whom everything was possible'
(Hennessy 1989, p.120). They came back from the War to
implement the Beveridge Report, and they all believed in it.
They believed in the mixed economy, with a Welfare State
that was going to be the syringer of tensions in society. It
would work its way through gradually, with improved
health, education and welfare, improved industrial relations
– the benign cycle that a combination of full employment, a
Keynesian notion as they would have said in those days, and
the Beveridge Report was going to produce this stable and
just society. And when these civil servants were coming up
to their last jobs in the 1970s, it all began to fall apart in the
winters of discontent and industrial strife of a very acute kind.
The consensus of which they were the human embodiment,
in terms of trying to make it work for ministers, began to
crumble all around them. They felt this very deeply, this
generation for whom everything was possible. They became
crisis managers, and the things they cared most about began
to fray in front of them.

I have a suspicion that we will have an equivalent
generation of those who made the European partnership
work and had come to believe in it, quite rightly because
ministers wanted them to, who now have to do the exit,

the dismantling, with multiple uncertainties, and it must be psychologically terribly hard for them to do that. If the Institute can be the place where they can talk about this in private, and if the Institute can help through discussions about the nature of public service, the ethic of it, I think that will be all to the good, and if I was in these civil servants' position, I'd want that, I really would.

CLAIRE FOSTER-GILBERT

That has been our experience of the civil servants we have spoken to, but not perhaps with quite that level of self-awareness: perhaps they do not want to look too hard at it because it is too painful. What is so impressive is the braced readiness to continue to carry out the will of ministers, to make the new policies and the new visions work, whether they agree with them or not. They do it because the minister has been democratically elected and they are supporting the democratic principle. But what is that? What is our *demos*, to go back to your first observations about the family members we do not recognize any more? What does democracy mean now? What is this thing that civil servants are sacrificing themselves for?

PETER HENNESSY

Votes prevail. That is the deal in this country. Raised voices: yes; raised fists: no. That is why Parliaments exist. That the raised fist is absolutely out of the question depends absolutely upon votes being respected, outcomes being respected.

If you are a senior civil servant now you will have started in Mrs Thatcher's day, and you will have seen several prime ministers and several ideological shifts. Over this time there has been the moral conscience question for some people in terms of wars. If you dip into the Chilcot enquiry (Committee of Privy Counsellors 2016), you will see how difficult it was for officials who had grave doubts about the process, not just the Iraq War itself, but also the process of decision-taking, which is illuminated in the Report in all its inadequacies, in technicolour. So the senior civil service – and not just the senior ranks – has gone through a lot already. But the Brexit shift is special. Most civil servants did not expect to face it when they went to bed, if they went to bed, that night on 23 June 2016. On the morning of 24 June they realized their world was changing. There would be a resetting of the dials on nearly all the fronts they could think of, and it must be terribly difficult for them. Now we should not get this out of perspective. It is not like war. People are not going to die because of Brexit, and there are not going to be military operations because of Brexit, for all the anxieties about a resurgent Russia and a weakened EU. So it is not like peace and war, but it is still pretty fundamental. The automatic pilots that public servants have been operating on, very well in many cases, are all in the process of altering or ceasing. It will be seven years at least before we achieve a final treaty. So if you are in your fifties now, you will be spending perhaps the last seven years of your professional life unravelling something you spent most of your professional life ravelling. That is an awfully long time to do something that worries you, with the multiple uncertainties created by the circumstances.

But the extended family theme – what is that? It is the people who breathe and work and love and die within the configuration of the UK. And that UK is up for question. The Scottish question is opened up even more by Brexit.

I'm in my 70th year now, and for my generation it is almost inconceivable that the UK would be no more, that I was born as a Brit, but I will die as a RUK: 'Remainder of the UK' (as the shrunken Kingdom is described in government white papers). I am not going to die a RUK. I find this extremely difficult to cope with. It is not because I am a drum-and-trumpet romantic about the nation, but I do love the place and I love every part of it – all the constituent regions and nations. And I find it difficult to contemplate that before I am much older we are going to lose Scotland, with all that Scotland has contributed, out of all proportion to the size of its population, to public and political service. More than that, to the thinking above our weight in the world, and the inventing above our weight in the world and the spying above our weight in the world, if you want to know the truth: Scotland produced some amazing operators in that world, as well as the military. I find this extremely difficult. For me, that bit of the emotional geography we are facing is more destabilizing than the European one, although I was a Remainer.

There are so many things to worry about. NATO is another thing to worry about. The United States. This is sounding like an encounter group, which I do not mean it to be. But if you get people to bring their anxieties to the table, the Institute's table, that of itself is a very great service. Because they all work very hard and don't have time to talk to each other about this. Civil servants may know what people in their sections think but they will not appreciate how people in other sections feel, because they do not have time, or the place, to talk to each other, and nor do the other institutions around Parliament Square. The judiciary and the two Houses of Parliament can be part of the conversation through the Institute, and that means that the moving parts of the state can talk to each other in ways they are not encouraged to by the system. That alone is enough to justify the existence of the Institute. Now if the Rule of St Benedict, on which Rowan Williams and others in this volume draw, could prevail... I am not a prohibitive person but if I could ban management consultants for at least three years having anything to do with the state, and replace them with a requirement that everybody should read the Rule of St Benedict... It is the best piece of management consultancy ever written. It is also the oldest piece of management consultancy ever written, and thanks to St Benedict's genius, we hit gold first time.

CLAIRE FOSTER-GILBERT

Is there a danger that 'stability' becomes an excuse for not looking beyond one's own local horizon, not noticing what is happening in the wider world?

PETER HENNESSY

That is not true stability. Most people most of the time think about family and friendship and pursuing a job or a profession that is worthwhile, a profession that is more than the sum of its parts. The stability of knowing that you are leading as decent a life as you can within your own family and personal relationships and that you are pursuing a profession that is worthwhile: that has a great tradition. Stability means feeling it is worthwhile getting out of bed on a wet Monday morning and coming into the office, because what you do is necessary. That is obvious in some professions such as nursing and teaching, but it is also true of public service. Public service is much more than just keeping the show on the road. It is making sure that people in public service do not put their hands in the till, and do not lie and do not deceive ministers. St Benedict's stability comes from having a tap root into a tradition. The public service tradition here is in a country that by and large has brought stability to the world, even though we are a destabilizing force at the moment because of Brexit. That is what matters to the hour-by-hour motivation of people trying to do a decent job. It is an ethic. It is is also about having a private life and a professional life that are not antipathetic to each other, as Vernon White notes; both express the kind of person you are, and of course they both shape you as well. Which is not to say that one shouldn't worry about the vicissitudes of liberal capitalism, of course one should, but not in permanent outrage about the state of liberal capitalism. Though some people are, and they make quite a lot of noise. There is something in what they say, to say the least.

CLAIRE FOSTER-GILBERT

Turning to my essays on growing moral courage, what would you say to the suggestion that it is not so much a matter of being good as of orienting ourselves on a journey to goodness, and what is important is the direction of travel?

PETER HENNESSY

The direction of travel is the key to it. It is not a case of having futile aspirations that are impossible; it is an incremental thing. It is the pride you get from doing a little bit better as you get older and think about it a bit more, and also what you transmit to the next generation coming through. That is a very good test of it; and there's something gone wrong if you transmit cynicism. So if you are jaded in the service of your profession, that is really corrosive. I am not advocating Dr Pangloss' refrain that all is for the best in the best of all possible worlds. I am suggesting that you can transmit the ennobling bits, not just the enabling bits, to successive generations, helping to form them in turn from all you have gained from your career over a lifetime in public service. You can never single out what you have contributed on your own in public service, but you did do the state some service. These are not lofty aspirations. There is just the quiet satisfaction that it has not all been in vain as you approach the final weeks before your retirement party, and most people would settle for that and it's an unheroic ethic but it's an ethic nonetheless. Vernon White refers to it when he quotes George Eliot's not making things 'so ill as they would have been'. There is no memorial to the 'unknown civil servant' in Westminster Abbey.

CLAIRE FOSTER-GILBERT

Perhaps there should be such an equivalent to the Grave of the Unknown Warrior.

What about politicians. Can the best of them be so inspired?

PETER HENNESSY

Yes. One of the big changes in my lifetime is the amount of casework MPs have to do in their constituency. For many of them, they tell me their greatest satisfaction is the difference they have made to their constituents. They might have shaped a law, they might have introduced a law that did actually produce a very significant change, and that will be their memorial, but it is those sloggy surgeries, the time you put in with sometimes quite difficult people, that made a big difference to those people. That produces a real satisfaction comparable to the teaching profession where you never know if you have helped. The job of the teacher is to light fires that kindle curiosity, so that, with Einstein, your pupils never lose a holy curiosity, they never forget. That is the single most important thing a teacher can do, and it is beyond the metrics of audits. That is the satisfaction when you totter into your retirement party or give your valedictory lecture that you have lit the fires of curiosity for a few people. Surely that is enough.

CLAIRE FOSTER-GILBERT

You seem to me to be describing Paul Ricoeur's concept of us all being *in medias res*, that is, we join the company of others for a while in our lifetimes, learning from those who have come before and from those whose company we keep, contributing what we can and being aware of the vast company of those who will follow us. We have just been singing 'For all the Saints' on account of it being All Saints Day, and the lines still catch in my throat:

> From earth's wide bounds, from ocean's farthest coast,
> Through gates of pearl streams in the countless host.

Each public servant contributes but they are in excellent and vast company, even if they don't always know about each other.

PETER HENNESSY

The armed forces, the security forces and the police understand the importance of continuity. In each generation they arc the ones who put themselves between us and danger, never knowing whether it is going to be terminal. Remembrance Day is public service in uniform day. There are regimental histories and their equivalents across the services so that each knows their great figures of the past and can identify with them in their own willingness to be exposed to danger, with the same motivation to great bravery of 'looking after your mates'.

CLAIRE FOSTER-GILBERT

You are describing a continuity of spirit.

What, now, of the conversation between Mary McAleese and the Dean, in which she speaks about the importance of interrogating one's own failings? Her observation that we seem to know nothing of our own failings but have doctorates in each other's reminds me of Sir Tom Philips' advice you cited earlier – to find out the thing of which a country and a people are least aware. It also echoes the Sermon on the Mount injunction to remove the beam in your own eye before attending to the mote in your neighbour's.

PETER HENNESSY

The eloquence of Mary's conversation with the Dean is very striking, and she captures states of mind brilliantly, including what it takes to get out of deep-set historical views of antagonisms and rights and slights. She is also very candid about her own pattern of thought and how it developed.

CLAIRE FOSTER-GILBERT

We could say that this willingness to interrogate one's own position was a sacrifice and a price that had to be paid to bring about the necessary Peace Process. What gives a people or a nation the courage to look at itself?

PETER HENNESSY

Sometimes it has to be an event that shocks you and brings you up short, which is regrettable. In one of the official histories of the home front of the Second World War, a senior civil servant expressed the view that few in Whitehall could have expected everyone to pull together so effectively for a greater cause, because of the social and economic strife of the 1920s and 30s. And yet the home front was mobilized quickly and the draconian laws to enforce it were hardly ever invoked because they were not needed: people did it anyway. And the War Cabinet that Churchill created was a coalition, each member of which was crucial to success, particularly the Labour members, Attlee and Greenwood, at the end of May 1940 when they backed Churchill in his determination not to seek a negotiated peace with Germany.

CLAIRE FOSTER-GILBERT

It matters politically to have the right people in the room.

PETER HENNESSY

Yes. If it had gone the other way and there had been a negotiated settlement with Hitler, history would have been so different for this country and a lot of other countries. That time is the hinge of the twentieth century. So it's a great shame that it seems to take shocks to make us take a serious look at ourselves. Maybe Brexit will turn out to be that. As we are talking now, in the autumn of 2016, the vocabulary of British politics is changing. It may be that the standard model of British politics, which is liberal capitalism jostling with social democracy, with the electorate sometimes voting for a serious squirt of one rather than the other but most of the time wanting the best bits of both – that may change. Scotland may leave the UK, and that will change things, although Labour has already lost its gold and dollar reserves of seats in Scotland. It is going to be very difficult for a centre-left government to form in England and Wales unless the centre left realigns itself and we get proportional representation for elections to Westminster.

The danger is that there are so many moving parts that everyone is confused. Confusion can lead to a degree of pessimism and sheer fatigue. Then we are in danger of indulging in what psychologists call 'cognitive shortcuts': cutting through all the complexities to find primary-coloured solutions and arguments. That is quite dangerous really.

But coming back to where we began, it is a wonderful thing to have within just a few hundred yards of all these felt uncertainties an institution that is older than all of the others, that can host the thoughts of them all. That is terribly important because if you cannot chat, first, and think, and pool thoughts, with a degree of candour, then opportunities will be lost in over-simplifying matters. I am aware of the danger of thinking that what happens around Parliament Square is an expression of what happens in the country; it is not that, but it is a crucial bit of the country, and if this bit of the country is not working, the rest of the country is not going to work either.

CLAIRE FOSTER-GILBERT

What of Vernon White's argument that idealism and morality and purposefulness do not go away in us, despite endless knockings back? Does this help orient us? It promises no simple or absolute solutions but it does stretch our moral and spiritual fibres beyond what we can see.

PETER HENNESSY

This is the virtue of hope. When we think about what we humans are: we are 90 per cent water; that statistic always brings me up short, being one of nature's wets, but here we are, these sentient beings who have done extraordinary things for good and bad, overall for good I think, the human race... well who knows, you cannot audit these things...but deeply innately within human beings is a chunk of hope, despite everything. Humour is an expression of this, the irony of it, the dark humour; in periods of difficulty that is a version of hope. The Christian churches all stress hope but it is not just in the Christian churches, it is innate within human beings. But the working through of hope requires chat, and that is what the Institute is for, usually of a very high order, and also it is about friendships, because friendships are made in the course of these chats, and these things matter, and they are all completely beyond measurement. Setting outcome measures, terrible words that come out from between clenched dentures in my case, for what the Institute does is impossible, because all the things that matter are beyond measurement.

CLAIRE FOSTER-GILBERT

The Institute is the place where public servants can do incommensurable, invaluable things, things you cannot count because you do not have to prove anything as a result of those conversations. But you can feel the difference in yourself. And you can find friends to whom you can return.

On this essay, could we pick up Andrew Tremlett's essay about communities being intentional, hardworking and sacrificial? Community is altogether more than something you identify with as a default, like being a vegetarian. Rather, you form it and it forms you. It requires sacrifice but it is also hugely rewarding, getting the right people around the table.

PETER HENNESSY

Intentionality is an interesting thought, because quite often the institutions we have been talking about exist to keep the show on the road and a lot of their work is just that: a decent justice system; a decent public administration raising taxes clearly and cleanly, ensuring the state only spends them on things that Parliament has specifically voted for... The maintenance job is very big indeed, and all that is high purpose too. Can you add intentionality that does not just take you into the intangibles? It is the curse of the age of management consultancies that they have reduced what institutions are for to a series of checklists that are almost entirely devoid of poetry. There is no hope in a management consultant's report is there? There is just exhortation of a crude kind.

CLAIRE FOSTER-GILBERT

This is where Vernon White's moral energy is diverted to when it has no other outlet – into measuring and criticizing the lack of accountability and efficiency. The sterile anger of that contrasts greatly with the poetry of the Rule, which begins, 'Listen carefully, my child...incline the ear of thy heart': a powerful call.

PETER HENNESSY

'Only those institutions are loved which touch the imagination', as R. H. Tawney (1917) put it. Poetry is squeezed out with excessive plumbing. Intentionality is a test, and it can reintroduce poetry. What is the institution really for? Can it be more effective at doing that thing, more explicit about it? Institutions should ask, with Sir Tom, what is that activity of which it is least self-aware, more than just keeping the show on the road?

CLAIRE FOSTER-GILBERT

The self-awareness is helped by asking each other. For example, we can see each other's unconscious biases even if we cannot see our own, and if we are friends we can tell each other.

And what of the issue I raise about being ready to move with a paradigm shift? The point made in the essay is that the first conversion is often the enemy of the second conversion, that is to say, once we are convinced that something is absolutely necessary to our existence, like oil or penicillin, we cannot imagine a world functioning without it, and so we simply do not see new possibilities when they show themselves. The Benedictine habit of retuning each day to the eternal makes it possible to see things differently.

PETER HENNESSY

I do think the standard model might be about to change, because of the uncertainties of Brexit and the survival of the Kingdom as a UK. As we are speaking this morning there will be a scientist somewhere who after years of working patiently at the laboratory bench has seen a juxtaposition that could take her to Scandinavia for a Nobel prize and change medicine. That is an easy example of what Aldous Huxley wrote, that life is routine punctuated by orgies.

CLAIRE FOSTER-GILBERT

But the civil servant *in medias res* is playing his part, quietly keeping the show on the road with that intentionality about it and awakeness in the middle of it, ready for change when it needs to come.

PETER HENNESSY

It is harder to trace the extraordinariness there. We historians concentrate on the primary-colour moments, like Mrs Thatcher coming to be prime minister in May 1979. Ours can be, wrongly, the Tommy Cooper analysis, that it's all like this and then suddenly it's all like that. It never is just like that. Politicians, too, are always claiming the language of transformation.

CLAIRE FOSTER-GILBERT

Which devalues the currency...

PETER HENNESSY

Enoch Powell once said that the job of politicians is to give the people a tune to hum. He is right – you have to learn how to communicate as a politician, but that tends to bring over-simplification. The language of transformation needs watching in public and political life because it leads to disappointment and disillusion. Overselling is one of the besetting temptations of the politician. It is not heroic to get up and say: I offer you modest incrementalism over a reasonable period of time.

CLAIRE FOSTER-GILBERT

The politicians could try and find a better way of saying just that. Because making a promise you are not going to keep, and doing it over and over again, is corrosive of trust. Are politicians forced to do this because they think it is what the population wants?

PETER HENNESSY

The danger comes when they inhale their own myth. They think because it is they who have come into office, it is all going to work this time. Some people inhale their own legend in advance even before they've created one, we've all got a version of that, we're all engaged in the writing of our own obituaries.

CLAIRE FOSTER-GILBERT

Perhaps there has to be a bit of that, a bit of self-aggrandizement, a bit of ambition, but it should be the spur, as Polonius says, on your heel, not on your forehead where it would look silly.

Do you have any final thoughts?

PETER HENNESSY

The simple line on all this is if Westminster Abbey, with all its great tradition, can give people the chance to chat in groups and thought pattern configurations that would not normally happen in the course of their professional lives, that is a great thing. And very Anglican. The threnodies that run right through this book are the ones of stability, intentionality and purpose and as high a level of self-awareness as you can possibly manage. I think that's enough, don't you?

AFTERWORD

Stephen Lamport

When the Westminster Abbey Institute was established three years ago, it was something of a gamble. We had done much careful research and preparation. There was a clear notion of what the Institute was intended – and not intended – to be. But clarity of purpose went hand in hand with the uncertainty of hope. To nurture and revitalize moral and spiritual values in public life are noble aspirations. But would they touch any sense of need or hunger in the world beyond the walls of the Abbey?

Three years later we have at least a partial answer. The challenges that confront those in all forms of public service have continued to grow in a world that, even in this short space, has become more fractured and uncertain. The pressure on its servants to meet the expectations and demands of the public, its political leaders and society at large has increased. The requirement to meet the highest standards of moral behaviour, or at least show unimpeachable conformity to an insatiable insistence on 'correctness' at the bar of public opinion, has set complex and often confusing demands on those who have dedicated themselves to serving the public good. Preserving confidence in one's ability to advise and work within a clear ethical framework is not easy in those circumstances. It needs recognition, support and encouragement. These are qualities that underpin the good governance of a genuinely civilized society. But they cannot be taken for granted. They need to be cherished and nurtured.

It is in this world that the Abbey Institute has found itself able to respond to a need. Its contribution is fed by a mixture of qualities. The Abbey's Benedictine identity and legacy provide a firm conviction of the imperative of service to others. The stability of the Abbey as a Christian institution that has endured the buffeting of centuries provides a point of certainty and solace in a changing and unpredictable world. The Abbey's reputation and profile enable it to attract to its sacred beauty the widest variety of people at all levels of society. It can provide a safe space for conversation and ideas, for error and enlightenment, of a kind increasingly difficult to find in a world where genuinely open debate is often hard to defend. And its unique position in the public square of institutional service embracing law, executive and legislature, with monarchy just down the road, gives it a place in the forum of public debate that needs no justification.

Will the need that the Institute has identified last? Like the Abbey of which it is an integral part, the Institute takes a long view of social and political need. It is not a think-tank lobbying to change policies from a particular political viewpoint. It does not exist to identify the answers and to find a constituency willing to embrace them. It is rather a listener, an encourager of others to look afresh from an ethical – and, yes, Christian – viewpoint with the aim of understanding their actions and re-identifying the basis of right action. Our belief is that this fills an important gap among the many who work to serve those around them, and that the need the Institute exists to address will continue to sit at the heart of the quest to construct a genuinely civilized society.

The essays in this collection will have, we hope, provided a glimpse into some of those ways in which the Institute can make a valuable contribution.

REFERENCES

Aintree University Hospitals NHS Foundation Trust (Respondent) v James (Appellant) [2013] Supreme Court of the United Kingdom.

Aquinas, T. (1975) *Summa Contra Gentiles*. Trans. V. J. Bourke. London: University of Notre Dame Press. (Original work published thirteenth century.)

Arendt, H. (1998) *The Human Condition*. Chicago: University of Chicago Press. (Original work published 1958.)

Barnes, J. (2009) *A History of the World in 10½ Chapters*. London: Vintage. (Original work published 1989.)

Barnes, J. (2011) *The Sense of an Ending*. London: Jonathan Cape.

Bauman, Z. (2000) *Liquid Modernity*. Oxford: Polity Press.

Beer, G. (2000) *Darwin's Plots: Evolutionary Narrative in Darwin, George Eliot and Nineteenth-Century Fiction*. Cambridge: Cambridge University Press.

Benedict (2016) *The Rule of Benedict*. London: Penguin Classics. (Original work published c. sixth century.)

Bentham, J. (1962) 'An Introduction to the Principles of Morals and Legislation'. In M. Warnock (ed.) *Utilitarianism*. Glasgow: William Collins Sons and Co. (Original work published 1789.)

Bolt, R. (1960) *A Man for all Seasons*. Premiered Globe Theatre.

Campbell, J. (1968) *The Hero with a Thousand Faces*. Princeton, NJ: Princeton University Press. (Original work published 1949.)

Cavanaugh, W. (2001) 'Stan the Man'. In Berkman, J. and Cartwright, M. (eds) *The Hauerwas Reader.* Durham, NC: Duke University Press.

Chittister, J. (2010) *The Rule of St Benedict: A Spirituality for the 21st Century.* New York: Crossroad Publishing Company. (Original work published 1992.)

Chryssavgis, J. (2003) *Cosmic Grace: Humble Prayer: The Ecological Vision of the Green Patriarch Bartholemew I.* Cubao, Philippines: Wm B Eerdmans Publishing Co.

Committee of Privy Counsellors (2016) *The Report of the Iraq Enquiry.* London: House of Commons.

Committee on Standards in Public Life (CSPL) (1995) *The Seven Principles of Public Life.* London: CSPL.

Critchley, S. (2007) *Infinitely Demanding: Ethics of Commitment, Politics of Resistance.* London: Verso.

Delanty, G. (2003) *Community.* London: Routledge.

Descartes, R. (1970) 'Discourse on the Method of Rightly Conducting the Reason and Seeking for Truth in the Sciences.' In *The Philosophical Works of Descartes.* Cambridge: Cambridge University Press. (Original work published 1637.)

De Waal, E. (1999) *Seeking God: The Way of St Benedict.* Norwich: Canterbury Press. (Original work published 1984.)

Donne, J. (2012) *The Best of John Donne.* CreateSpace Independent Publishing Platform.

Eliot, G. (1965) *Middlemarch.* Harmondsworth: Penguin. (Original work published 1871–2.)

Eliot, T. S. (1969) 'Gerontion.' In *The Complete Poems and Plays of T. S. Eliot.* London: Faber. (Original work published 1920.)

Fergusson, N. (2015) *Kissinger 1923–1968: The Idealist.* London: Penguin.

Flores, F. and Gray, J. (2000) *Entrepreneurship and the Wired Life.* London: Demos.

Foster, C. (2001) *The Ethics of Medical Research on Humans.* Cambridge: Cambridge University Press.

Fox, M. (2000) *Original Blessing: A Primer in Creation Spirituality.* New York: Jeremy P. Tarcher/Putnam.

Francis, Pope (2015) *Laudato Si'.* Vatican: Vatican Press.

Giddens, A. (1991) *Modernity and Self-Identity.* Cambridge: Polity Press.

Gray, J. (2003) *Straw Dogs*. London: Granta Books.

Gray, J. (2007) *Black Mass: Apocalyptic Religion and the Death of Utopia*. London: Penguin.

Hague, W. (2005) *William Pitt the Younger: A Biography*. London: HarperCollins.

Hague, W. (2008) *William Wilberforce: The Life of a Great Anti-Slave Campaigner*. London: HarperCollins.

Heidegger, M. (1977) *The Question Concerning Technology and Other Essays*. Trans. W. Lovitt. London: Harper and Row.

Hemingway, E. (1940) *For Whom the Bell Tolls*. New York: Charles Scribner's Sons.

Hennessy, P. (1989) *Whitehall*. London: Secker & Warburg.

Hennessy, P. (2014) *Establishment and Meritocracy*. London: Haus Curiosities.

Herriot, P. and Pemberton, C. (1995) *New Deals: The Revolution in Managerial Careers*. Chichester: John Wiley.

HMSO (2005) *Mental Capacity Act*. London: HMSO.

Hughes, N. and White, H. (2016) *Ministers Reflect: On Parliament*. London: Institute for Government.

James, P. (2012) *Sustainable Communities, Sustainable Development*. Melbourne: Institute of Post-Colonial Studies.

Jaspers, C. (1952) *Tragedy is not Enough*. Boston: Beacon Press.

Kant, I. (1985) *Fundamental Principles of the Metaphysic of Morals*. Trans. T. K. Abbott. New York: Prometheus Books. (Original work published 1785.)

Kant, I. (2012) *On a Supposed Right to Tell Lies from Benevolent Motives*. New York: SophiaOmni. (Original work published 1797.)

Kaufman, G. (1997) *How to be a Minister*. London: Faber and Faber. (Original work published 1980.)

Kennedy, I. (1980) 'If I were you, Mrs B.' *Reith Lectures*. Available at http://downloads.bbc.co.uk/rmhttp/radio4/transcripts/1980_reith4.pdf, accessed on 30 December 2016.

Keynes, J. M. (1923) *A Tract on Monetary Reform*. London: Macmillan.

Kissinger, H. (2015) *World Order*. New York: Penguin Books.

Kundera, M. (2000) *The Unbearable Lightness of Being*. London: Faber & Faber.

Lambeth (1998) *Transformation and Renewal: The Official Report of the Lambeth Conference*. London: Morehouse Publishing.

Lawrence, D. H. (1994) *Complete Poems*. Ware: Wordsworth Editions Ltd.

Lipsey, R. (2013) *Hammarskjöld: A Life*. Ann Arbor, MI: University of Michigan Press.

London Policing Ethics Panel (2014) *Ethical Challenges of Policing in London*. London: MOPAC.

McGilchrist, I. (2009) *The Master and his Emissary: The Divided Brain and the Making of the Western World*. New Haven, CT: Yale University Press.

MacIntyre, A. (1981) *After Virtue*. London: Duckworth.

McNeill, J. R. (2000) *Something New Under the Sun: An Environmental History of the Twentieth-Century World*. London: Penguin Books.

Marcel, G. (1949) *Being and Having*. Westminster: E. T. Dacre.

Margalit, A. (2010) *On Compromise*. Princeton, NJ: Princeton University Press.

Martin, J. (2007) *The Meaning of the 21st Century: A Vital Blueprint for Ensuring our Future*. London: Random House.

Moriarty, C. (2006) *Values and Values Conflict in the Civil Service*. London: Department for Transport.

Neruda, P. (1979) *The Poetry of Pablo Neruda*. Cambridge, MA: Harvard University Press.

Oborne, P. (2007) *The Triumph of the Political Class*. London: Simon and Schuster.

Oliver, M. (1986) 'Wild Geese'. In *Dream Work*. New York: Atlantic Monthly Press.

Page, W. (1909) *Benedictine Monks: St Peter's Abbey, Westminster*. London: Victoria County History.

Ricoeur, P. (1975) 'Phenomenology and Hermeneutics.' *Nous* 9, 85–102.

Royce, J. (1908) *The Philosophy of Loyalty*. New York: Macmillan.

Sachs, J. (2013) *To Move the World: JFK's Quest for Peace*. New York: Random House.

Stacey, J. (1990) *Brave New Families*. New York: Basic Books.

Tawney, R. H. (1917) 'A National College of All Souls.' *Times Educational Supplement*, 22 February.

Temple, W. (1956) *Christianity and the Social Order*. London: Penguin Books Ltd.

Tönnies, F. (1957) *Gemeinschaft und Gesellschaft*. East Lansing: Michigan State University Press. (Original work published 1887.)

Underhill, E. (2000) *Practical Mysticism*. London: General Publishing Co Ltd. (Original work published 1914.)

Weil, S. (2001) *Waiting for God*. London: Perennial Classics.

White, V. (2015) *Purpose and Providence: Taking Soundings in Western Thought, Literature and Theology*. London: Bloomsbury.

Whyte, D. (2015) *How Corrupt is Britain?* London: Pluto Press.

Williams, B. (2014) *Essays and Reviews 1959–2002*. Princeton, NJ: Princeton University Press.

Williams, R. (2000) *Lost Icons: Reflections on Cultural Bereavement*. Edinburgh: T&T Clark.

Williamson, H. (1969) *The Gale of the World*. London: Faber and Faber.

Wilson, E. O. (2001) *The Diversity of Life*. London: Penguin Books.

Zizioulas, J. (1990) 'Preserving God's Creation III: Three Lectures on Theology and Ecology.' *King's Theological Review XIII*, 1.

AUTHOR BIOGRAPHIES

Claire Foster-Gilbert

Claire Foster-Gilbert read theology at Balliol College, Oxford. She was a Research Fellow at King's College, publishing *The Ethics of Medical Research on Humans* (CUP 2001), developing and teaching an intellectual framework for the ethical scrutiny of medical research and working with the Department of Health to create a comprehensive network of ethics committees across the UK. Claire then became adviser in medical ethics and environmental issues for the Church of England, where she published *Sharing God's Planet* (CHP 2005); *How many lightbulbs does it take to change a Christian* (CHP 2007), and *Don't stop at the lights* (CHP 2008). Claire became a lay Canon at St Paul's Cathedral and in 2003 co-founded St Paul's Institute, where she co-edited a book of Rowan Williams' dialogues on global issues *The Worlds We Live In* (DLT 2005). In 2008 she founded a charity, The Ethics Academy, and published *Hero's Journal* (The Ethics Academy, 2009), a programme teaching moral strength and courage to young people and adults through the story of the 'hero's journey'. Westminster Abbey Institute was established in 2013 with Claire as its founder Director. Claire continues to research and write on ecology and theology.

William Hague

Lord Hague was first elected to Parliament for the seat of Richmond, North Yorkshire, at a by-election in 1989. At 27 years old he was the youngest Conservative Member of Parliament. In 1994 he became Minister of State with responsibility for Social Security and Disabled People, and in 1995 he introduced the landmark Disability Discrimination Act. Prime Minister John Major appointed him Secretary of State for Wales in the same year making him, at 34, Britain's youngest cabinet minister since Harold Wilson in 1947.

Lord Hague became Leader of the Conservative Party after the 1997 General Election. He led his party to victory in the European elections of 1999 and was widely credited for leading a successful campaign against the country joining the Euro. He stood down as leader following the re-election of Tony Blair at the 2001 General Election, before being appointed as Foreign Secretary in 2010. During his tenure as Foreign Secretary he dealt with one of the most tumultuous periods in modern history with unrest across the Middle East, and crises in Europe. He set about reviving the Foreign and Commonwealth Office, opening new embassies in Latin America and Africa, expanding Britain's presence in China and India, re-opening the language school, establishing the Diplomatic Academy, and personally visiting 83 countries. In 2012 he launched the Preventing Sexual Violence Initiative with UN High Commissioner for Refugees, Angelina Jolie Pitt, to address the culture of impunity that exists for crimes of sexual violence in conflict, and increase the number of perpetrators held to account.

Lord Hague is currently chairing the United for Wildlife Taskforce which is tackling the trafficking of illegal wildlife products, as part of a collaboration of seven conservation organisations and The Royal Foundation. In March 2016 he was made an Honorary Fellow of Magdalen College, Oxford.

John Hall

The Very Reverend Dr John Hall was installed as the 38th Dean of Westminster on 2nd December 2006, and is responsible for the mission, ministry and maintenance of Westminster Abbey. Brought up in South London, he taught in Kenya, read Theology at Durham and, after two years teaching RE in Hull, was ordained in 1975 and served in three parishes in South London. From 1992 he was Director of Education for the Diocese of Blackburn. From 1998 until his appointment as Dean, he served as the Church of England's Chief Education Officer, responsible for the Church's strategy and policy in relation to church schools and education generally. He has been a governor of many schools and two universities and a trustee of many charitable trusts. He is a Fellow of the Society of Antiquaries and of the Royal Society of Arts, of Canterbury Christ Church University, and of St Chad's College in the University of Durham and an honorary Fellow of the College of Teachers and the University of Wales Trinity Saint David. He is a Companion of St Dunstan's Educational Foundation and has honorary doctorates from the Universities of Roehampton, Chester, Westminster and Hull. He is an honorary liveryman of the Worshipful Company of Educators and is a Pro Chancellor of the University of Roehampton.

Peter Hennessy

Lord Hennessy is Attlee Professor of Contemporary British History at Queen Mary University of London, and an independent crossbench peer in the House of Lords.

Stephen Lamport

Sir Stephen Lamport has been Receiver General of Westminster Abbey and Chapter Clerk since 2008. Stephen read History at Cambridge from 1970–1973, and International Relations at the University of Sussex from 1973–1974. He joined the Foreign & Commonwealth Office in 1974 and served at the UK's Mission to the United Nations, and at the British Embassies in Tehran and Rome. While at the Foreign Office he co-authored a novel, *The Palace of Enchantments*, with Douglas Hurd. He was appointed Deputy Private Secretary to The Prince of Wales in February, 1993, then Private Secretary and Treasurer, from 1996 to 2002. From 2002 to 2007 he was a Group Director of the Royal Bank of Scotland.

Mary MacAleese

Dr Mary McAleese was President of Ireland from 1997 until 2011. She was the first President to come from Northern Ireland. Born in Belfast in 1951, she grew up as the eldest of nine children in Ardoyne, a sectarian flashpoint area of the city, and experienced first-hand the violence of The Troubles. Her family home was machine-gunned and the family business was bombed by Loyalist paramilitaries.

The theme of her presidency was Building Bridges, and her work for peace and reconciliation culminated in the historic state visit to Ireland by H.M. Queen Elizabeth II in May 2011. A barrister and journalist by training, she was Reid Professor at Trinity College Dublin, Director of the Institute of Professional Legal Studies at Queen's University and

Queen's first female pro-Vice Chancellor. She worked as a journalist in Irish radio and television. She was a co-founder of Belfast Women's Aid, the Campaign for Homosexual Law Reform, the Irish Commission for Prisoners Overseas and Co-Chair of the Working Party on Sectarianism set up by the Irish Council of Churches and the Catholic Church. She is the author of *Reconciled Being: Love in Chaos* (1997), *Building Bridges* (2011) and *Collegiality in the Code of Canon Law* (2014).

Since leaving office in 2011, Mary has studied at the Pontifical Gregorian University in Rome. There she has obtained a Licentiate in Canon Law, and is currently completing a doctorate on children's rights in canon law. She chaired the European Commission's High Level Group on the Modernisation of Third Level Education, and has been a Visiting Professor at Boston College, the University of Notre Dame and St. Mary's University Twickenham. Mary is married to Martin since 1976. They have three adult children and two grandsons.

Andrew Tremlett

The Very Reverend Andrew Tremlett has been the Dean of Durham since July 2016. Prior to that, Andrew served as a Curate in Torquay from 1989 to 1992 and then Chaplain to the Mission to Seafarers, and Assistant Chaplain to the Anglican Church in Rotterdam, the Netherlands. From 1995 to 1998 he was a Parliamentary Research Assistant and Secretary to the Church of England's Doctrine Commission. He then became Canon Residentiary and Keeper of the Fabric at Bristol Cathedral, where he was Acting Dean.

From 2010 to 2016 Andrew was Rector of St Margaret's Church at Westminster Abbey, where he was responsible for the Abbey's relationships with Parliament, Whitehall and other faith communities, and in 2012 he established the Westminster Abbey Institute, working with Public Service

Institutions and Parliament Square to support ethics in public life. In June 2014 he became Archdeacon of Westminster and Sub-Dean of the Abbey. From 2013 to 2016 he was Chairman of the Field Lane Foundation, a charitable housing association working particularly with adults with complex needs, and in 2015 because a Trustee of the Mission to Seafarers. He is the President of St Cuthbert's Hospice in Durham and a member of the Council of the University of Durham.

Vernon White

The Reverend Professor Vernon White is Sub-Dean and Canon Theologian at Westminster Abbey, where he has particular responsibility for theological study and teaching, and is a member of the Institute steering group. He is also a Visiting Professor in Theology at King's College London. He has had a longstanding concern for both academic and public theology, and is the author of a number of academic books in the area of philosophical and moral theology, Christian doctrine, and social ethics. After studying at Cambridge and Oxford, he has held a variety of posts in Church and Academy, as a Parish Incumbent, Cathedral Chancellor, Chaplain and University Lecturer, and Principal of a Theological Training Institution. He was appointed to Westminster Abbey in 2011.

Rowan Williams

Lord Williams was born in Wales and studied theology in Cambridge and Oxford, pursuing research in Russian Orthodox thought. He has served for ten years as Bishop of Monmouth, and for another ten as Archbishop of Canterbury, and taught at several universities. Since retiring from Canterbury in 2012, he has been Master of Magdalene College, Cambridge. He has written many books on theology and spirituality, and has published a number of articles on Benedictine monasticism.

SUBJECT INDEX

AUTHOR INDEX